"Richard not only is a brilliant story teller, inspiring   he is a man who walks in the full authority of gut wrenching, stomach turning ability that only the truly prayer-led place their faith in. The world has been gifted this book to remind us once more, of not just the power of prayer, but the transformation of His kindness, His redemption, His majesty. Every page challenges us, it confronts those questions we're frightened to ask. That's the beauty of Richard's approach, his own experience answered these questions for us, and in pouring out his brutal honesty into these chapters, we are no longer walking in hopelessness, wondering if God will come through, we are renewed by the power of the hundreds of recorded stories that could have been pushed aside. I charge anyone to read this book, and not be fully inspired, convicted even, to not walk in the kind of faith that only the brave choose to walk in. His words will undo you, as they did me. An essential piece written by a wonderfully humble and humorous man, a piece that was clearly God ordained – for such a time as this."
Carrie Lloyd, author of The Noble Renaissance

"Reading 'remember' has been both refreshing and challenging. So many stories of answered prayer that will stir your faith. I love the very simple and practical steps Richard has shared to enable any believer to begin to value more than ever acts of God in their lives. This book is a huge blessing to the body of Christ."
James Aladiran, Founder, Prayer Storm

"Utterly inspiring! If you have ever doubted the power of prayer, just read this book. I loved it! This is the perfect book for anyone who wants to study the power of prayer on their own or in a group. It is brilliantly put together and utterly inspirational."
Rosemary Conley CBE

"Richard is a Kingdom mischief maker who tells stories with a cheeky smile and a glint in his eye that leaves the reader 'strangely warmed'. This is a book that ignites faith and is worth reading for the stories of answered prayer alone. It also contains depth and hard won insights made accessible through humour and humility that left me stirred to pray again for both the everyday things and the audacious. I hope many will read this book and discover the world also revolves around their personal faith adventure and a God who answers prayer."
Rich Wilson, Fusion Movement Leader

"A compelling and thought provoking read. There has never been a more important time for the Church to remember the almighty and prayer-answering God we follow. Richard has pressed through, persevered and is a living, breathing example of how faithful our God is…. and we all know that He does His things in His timing"

Dr John Kirkby CBE, Founder of Christians Against Poverty

"One thing I know without a shadow of doubt. Prayer has power. It always has. It always will. And it has now, in our everyday lives in our world today that is full of challenge and change. In fact, the rate of change is frightening in that technology brings new convenience, new opportunities, new science to every aspect of our lives. Perhaps it makes us feel more capable, answering each need, easing every task and thinking for us in so many ways.

But the future that technology brings can never change the truths of the past – the great mystery of life itself, created by God who gives us life, who is present in each of our days, and who knows our longings and our fears without us ever having to put them into words. But when we do pour out our hearts to him in prayer, He hears us because He knows us. And over my three decades of presenting the BBC Television series SONGS OF PRAISE, during which I've met and talked to hundreds of people who have been kind enough to share their experiences with me, I have come to know just how powerful prayer is. Whether millions of us pray together for a particular cause during a live SONGS OF PRAISE, or whether that prayer comes from one lone voice of despair in the depths of a dark night, God hears. And He answers – not always in the way we hope or expect, but according to His own will for us and for others.

Richard Gamble's life has been so positively led and guided through answered prayer. He is determined to encourage others to include prayer as a regular part of their lives, and to recognise when their prayers have been answered. Most important of all, he wants us to make a note of all those occasions and remember them – because recognising God's practical presence in our lives in the past is the most reassuring promise for the future.

I'd be surprised if you weren't moved to tears by this book. The stories are compelling, extraordinary, and deeply reassuring.

God is with us. Prayer has power. It always has. It always will. And it's here for us – all of us – today."

Pam Rhodes

Richard Gamble is the founder of Eternal Wall, a colossal architectural sculpture remembering a million answered prayers. He has had a wide and varied career, from building a successful software business to being chaplain of Leicester City (when they were rubbish), to picking out the bad crisps at a crisp factory. *Remember* is his debut book.

REMEMBER

Revealing the eternal power
of answered prayer

First published in Great Britain in 2018

Society for Promoting Christian Knowledge
36 Causton Street
London SW1P 4ST
www.spck.org.uk

British Library Cataloguing-in-Publication Data
A catalogue record for this book is available from the British Library

ISBN 978-0-281-08421-0
eBook ISBN 978-0-281-08422-7

3 5 7 9 10 8 6 4 2

Typeset by Nord Compo
Printed and bound by CPI Group (UK) Ltd, Croydon CR0 4YY

First printed in Great Britain by Ashford Colour Press

eBook by Nord Compo

Produced on paper from sustainable forests

Sincere thanks to the baristas at Coventry Showcase Costa; without your unswerving commitment to caffeine delivery, none of this would have been possible.

Contents

A passion to remember

Only be careful, and watch yourselves closely so that you do not forget the things your eyes have seen or let them fade from your heart as long as you live. Teach them to your children and to their children after them. (Deut. 4.9)

I REMEMBER one night that changed the course of my life for ever. I was 11 years old and had gone to my nan's for the night, which usually consisted of sitting in her front room watching *It's a Knockout*[1] on a small black-and-white TV and eating jam roly poly – but not that evening. The next-door neighbours were having an argument, prompting my mischievous nan to teach me a new trick: she took a glass out of the cabinet, licked her finger and ran it around the rim of the glass before putting it against the wall and starting to listen. She let me have a go, and soon we were taking it in turns to eavesdrop on her next-door neighbours' domestic! Though slightly disturbing to look back on it now, at the age of 11 it was great fun. Little did I know then what would happen the next time I tried the trick.

The following night, back at home, I decided to try out my new-found skill to earwig on Mum and Dad's conversation in the room next to mine. I licked my finger, ran it around the edge of the glass and placed it on the wall. *Wow, it works!* I closed my eyes to concentrate on what was being said and managed to pick out the words, 'I might have cancer . . . hospital test . . . tomorrow morning.' I sat on my bed, stunned by what my curiosity had stumbled upon, and I instinctively decided to pray. I was not brought up in a Christian home, and so my only experience of anything remotely spiritual had been watching the comedy *Bread*, where at the end of the episode, the guy would kneel by his bed, put his hands together and reel off his requests to God. Not knowing how to pray, I did the same – lights out, I knelt by the bed, hands together, and whispered into the darkness, 'Dear God, can you please look after my mum?'

It's difficult for me to explain what happened next, but I immediately sensed that God was in the room. It was sort of like having

---

1 *It's a Knockout* was a BBC show where the basic premise was to laugh at people competing against each other falling over, getting wet and generally looking stupid. As humanity has taken giant technological leaps forward in recent decades, we have now advanced to filming ourselves falling over, getting wet and generally looking stupid. Thus *It's a Knockout* was discontinued in 2001. You can't stop progress.

this huge hand wrap around me, comforting me. I felt warm, sort of fuzzy and safe, and like it was all going to be okay – and it was. I remember getting into my bed, not being worried any more, and falling asleep. I never mentioned what I heard to my mum, and as far as I can remember, I never worried about it again. I knew God had heard me.

Years later, I was to discover that what I had experienced was called 'the presence of God'. It was the beginning of my story, a pivotal moment, and from that point onwards, I always believed in him. God's existence was an unshakeable truth for me. In any discussions that followed at school or university, I would always fall on the side of defending God; even though I had no relationship with him, I knew he was there. It took a decade for me to find someone who could explain the gospel to me, or maybe it took a decade until I was ready to accept it. Either way, that moment as an innocent child was my first encounter with the God who lives, the God who listens and the God who answers.

Today, some 41 years later, following the quiet whisper of God's voice has led me on a mission to try to collect a million stories of answered prayer. Together, these will form the one million bricks of The Eternal Wall of Answered Prayer, a national monument that will seek to communicate to the visual age of the twenty-first century that Jesus is alive, he listens and he answers. I had, of course, heard stories from preachers and read accounts in books, but I wondered what other stories were out there? What stories of God's amazing work would I find?

The obvious place to start gathering these stories of answered prayer seemed to me to find those who were fervent about prayer, those who had a zeal for seeking God's face. Visiting over a hundred churches across different denominations and speaking to more than a thousand church and parachurch leaders, I found countless people committed to developing places and networks for the Church to build one-on-one relationships with the one who holds the universe in his hands. However, despite their enthusiasm for prayer, I found a common thread starting to emerge among their responses: they struggled to get their hands on these answered prayers.

This was surprising. Perhaps naively, I was expecting them to have reams of stories, catalogues of God's miracles, systems to capture every time he answered, so they could spur each other to engage with God even more. Instead, I discovered that it was often a struggle to recall what God had done in their ministries. Did it mean God wasn't answering prayers in these communities? Absolutely not. There was simply little spiritual muscle memory to recall these places in the past that were seemingly rarely revisited; many people I spoke to had to pause and think, searching the recesses of their minds for stories of answered prayer.

Naturally, there were other people who could regale story after story of God answering prayer in their lives; some church leaders, like Jarrod Cooper of the Revive Church in Hull, could even point to little booklets that captured some of the answered prayers within their congregation that could be given to new members. It was more common on my travels, however, to find people had to search harder to remember the stories that once inspired so much faith – so much so that I started to wonder: does it really matter? I uncovered some pretty jaw-dropping stories of God at work, and when I have shared these with others since, they seem to be encouraged and their faith built up. But does it stop there? Does it matter if these particular accounts never get told again? And yet, at the same time as having these encounters, I was finding myself becoming almost obsessed with the thematic thread of remembrance that runs through the Bible. The theme is so consistently present through most books in the Scriptures that I am convinced that the tradition of remembrance found in its pages must be of continued relevance for us today. So why do so many of us forget to remember what God has done and simply turn our attention and our prayer lives to what he might do next?

It is my absolute passion to remember what God has done,[2] and so, simply put, this book hopes to make some steps in restoring the seemingly lost art of remembering and in some way to narrow the gap between the prevalence of remembrance in God's word and our present-day practice. It will explore the importance of spiritual remembering and provide practical suggestions for how we might undertake it. It will investigate the power of stories of answered prayer and demonstrate that, when unlocked, they can transform not only the person in the story but anyone who cares to listen. As we set our sight on his acts in the past, our ability to win the challenges of the present will be strengthened, and our future with him will be ever brighter.

There are many examples in the Bible of how to remember the works of God's hand, many of which we'll explore in this book. One of them is, of course, written accounts, the Bible itself being the supreme example. Another one, lesser used today, is stones. In Joshua 4.20, we see that when the Israelites crossed the Jordan River, they erected 12 stones from the riverbed to remember God's mighty miracle for them. To get us into the habit of remembering, each chapter of this book will end with one of 11 stories of answered prayer to remind us of who God is: the God who lives, the God who listens and the God who answers.

Answered prayer: summer 1990

Mark was on holiday in Lanzarote when he hired a jeep for the day and decided to go off-roading over sand dunes. He figured this was way more exciting than sticking to the roads that were populated with slow buses and tourists on mopeds. With the adrenalin taking

---

2 I had considered having Isaiah 26 on my tombstone: 'The desire of our soul is for your name and the remembrance of you.' It was only on seeing the latter part of the scripture that I decided to give it a miss: 'We have, as it were, brought forth wind' (NKJV).

hold, he flew over a dune without seeing the significant drop on the other side. Soon, the jeep was nose-diving into deep sand, hidden to any passing traffic. No matter how hard he tried, the jeep was stuck – he was stranded. So he prayed. He prayed earnestly for someone to come and rescue him. Within a few short minutes, two figures approached and asked if he needed help. They cheerfully proceeded to dig out enough sand so that he could start the jeep and get it moving again. Mark asked them how they knew he was there. The answer surprised him as much as their rescue: 'We saw a flash of light coming from your direction and were prompted to go and see what it was.' *Did the light bounce off the jeep?* Mark wondered. But no, it was buried deep. Mark drove back to his villa, figuring that God had heard his prayer and thanking him for his rescue, all the while repenting for driving like a numpty. Little did Mark know that God had rescued people from the sands before . . .

Diana was on holiday with friends on the Greek island of Rhodes in the 1970s and drove her hire car out onto the beach. Though initially fun, the error of her ways soon became apparent as the sand softened and the car became completely stuck. She looked around for people to help, but no one was about. This was in the days before mobile phones, and so no one knew where they were. Panic started to set in before Diana said, 'I think we should pray and ask God for help.' No sooner had they finished praying, they looked up and saw a huge man wearing camouflage gear coming towards them. He said nothing, bent down and lifted the car out of the soft sand and placed it where they could drive again. When they turned to thank him, he disappeared as mysteriously as he had come. Diana is convinced to this day that God sent her an angel.

Part 1

WHY REMEMBER?

1
Have we forgotten
to remember?

I fear the day when technology overlaps our humanity. It will be then that the world will have permanent ensuing generations of idiots. (Unknown[1])

---

1   You'll see that the fact that the internet widely *incorrectly* attributes this quote to Albert Einstein rather emphasizes the points I'm about to make in this chapter.

Through my teenage years, my mum and dad used to drive me mad when we watched TV. It was always the same routine. In the first few scenes, Mum would focus on one of the actors, and for the next thirty minutes, she and Dad would try their best to remember what film or programme he or she had featured in. 'Is it Ellen? Or was it Elaine?' Meanwhile, I'm getting the right hump because I just want to *watch* the episode; I pledge to myself that I will not do the same to my kids. Yet years later, I catch myself watching films and saying, 'Oh, where have I seen her before? What was she in?' Within seconds, my son is on his iPhone and into the IMDB app: 'It's Ruth Wilson; she was in *His Dark Materials*, *Luther* and *Saving Mr. Banks*.' End of discussion. Back to the plot.

Life is so different now with every piece of information at our fingertips. There is now no need to search the deep recesses of our memory – just google it for instant answers. Googling it is quicker and undoubtedly more accurate, so why bother remembering? I can programme my digital calendar to remember birthdays, Evernote can capture any task I need to do, and Facebook can pop up photo memories from five years ago of other people's brilliant holidays.[1] Any fact, TV clip or song is just a moment away from technological recall. So, what's the point in remembering any more when computer processing can do it far more effectively?

I'm not in any way a technophobe; I love the fact that reminiscing to the theme tune of *Bagpuss* or *Danger Mouse* is only a click away. I guess I'm not particularly keen on the constant factual corrections I get from my kids googling under the dinner table, but you can't have everything.[2] What are the ramifications of this instant data

---

1 I recognize there is concern around social media censorship, but, come on, could we at least all agree on a carpet ban of *those* holiday shots of empty beaches, stunning landscapes and private pools that make us all jealous?

2 Once when my son was moaning that he had to cycle seven miles to school, I explained I did the same when I was his age so he needs to just 'suck it up'. He then google mapped it and showed me my journey was only 4.3 miles! Information is king.

gratification and the relinquishing of our need to remember? Does it change the way we think? Does it change the way we act? Perhaps an even more important question: if we don't need to actively *remember* any more, should that also apply to our spiritual life?

The Google effect

Karl Ericsson's[I] theory is that it takes ten thousand hours to be world class at anything – a sort of scientific evidence for 'practice makes perfect'. The theory goes that each activity of our brain creates neural pathways and the more we do a particular thing, the stronger those pathways become and the better we become at it. The notion goes that if I practice for four hours a day for seven years, I will be able to operate at an elite level – so my chances of representing Great Britain in rhythmic dance at the 2028 Olympic Games are very much alive! Clearly, it's not that straightforward. But simply put, our brains have an inbuilt ability to increase the skill and effectiveness of a task the more frequently we do it. Conversely, the less we do a thing, the harder it becomes. It follows then that if our brain exercises less at remembering, our function and efficiencies of recall will be affected. Researching this question, Betsy Sparrow,[II] a psychologist from Columbia University, uncovered 'digital amnesia', also known as the 'Google effect'. Sparrow identified that the technological age was indeed changing the way we think, the way we remember and even our ability to do so. Her research found that as we 'google', or search for answers on the internet, our ability to remember the facts we uncover is greatly reduced. Those who use the internet more than books for information are significantly less likely to remember those facts. On the flip side, Sparrow found that these individuals had an enhanced ability to access information online; whatever information was needed, they were able to find it and find it quickly. They did not store it; rather, they were able to recall *how* to access it again, only the next time much quicker. This research feeds into the suspicions of Nicholas Carr, author of *Is Google Making Us Stupid*, that the internet is physically changing the way we think:

> Over the past few years I've had an uncomfortable sense that someone, or something, has been tinkering with my brain, remapping the neural circuitry, reprogramming the memory.

Now, before I go all Tolpuddle[3] on everyone, it is probably not surprising that we have been here before. The advent of the printing press caused many to be concerned over how books would change our culture. Fears were raised that it would have an impact on the oral traditions of storytelling and that these practices caused people to actually meditate on what they were hearing. The writing of Scriptures was seen as an aid to meditation, and the concern with printed reading was that it would only impart information at a shallow level. Fifteenth-century Benedictine abbot Trithemius was greatly troubled: 'He who ceases from zeal for writing because of printing is no true lover of the Scriptures.'[III] I wonder what he would make of us present-day Christians who listen to the word of God while they are driving to work. He also grumbled that printing presses would make his monks lazy as they no longer had to create the holy manuscripts. So, techno-panic is not new, and though I am a technology fan, it is important to focus on areas where the digital age is having an impact on culture in conflict with the Scriptures. One of the examples of this cultural impact is the erosion of transactive memory.

---

3 The Tolpuddle Martyrs' stand against the progress of industrialization is the *only* fact I can remember from my history 'O'-Levels. For more, see Google!

The eroding art of remembering

As I sat frustrated with my parents' trying to recall the actors on our 80s-style TV, they were actually demonstrating 'transactive memory'. The process was discovered by Daniel Wegner[IV] in 1985, who found that two people who knew each other well were able to recall significantly more than two strangers together with the same subject matter. The conclusion was that couples or groups had between them an external memory that they could access together that was greater than the sum of its parts. In other words, when Mum and Dad were searching for the actress's name, they were able to share with each other elements of information they could each recall, which enabled them to eventually get the right answer.[4] This process of remembering together meant that this information was more accessible, more memorable in the future, particularly because they had shared the cognitive process to arrive there together. The internet age has largely done away with this collective transactive memory among people, now replacing it with the largest external memory bank in history, with access for all. The advantages are significant – instant access and, aside from fake news, enhanced accuracy – but the loss of cognitive process in this change has a number of negative impacts:

1 Remembering facts and information is becoming less about an essential part of our being, nor are these facts aiding an individual towards deep learning. Remembering has become more about learning how to *get* to the information.
2 Remembering with others is no longer necessary, leading to independence and isolation of thought. Any relational benefits of shared cognitive processes are lost.

---

4   Usually at the most dramatic part of the episode.

3 Sparrow noted that as we search for the information we want online, we do so alone, missing out on processing the details. Opposing views or engaging in challenging conversations which may shape or soften our opinions are avoided, and consequently our views become more extreme.

What is more concerning for our faith, as we will explore in the next chapter, is the devaluation we are seeing, not only in remembering itself but in the history we recall. As Sparrow says, 'Obviously we need some baseline skill in memorizing things, but I personally have never seen all that much intellectual value in memorizing things.' In other words, don't bother learning Scripture when we can just google it or flick to our Bible apps. This worldview sees little benefit in retaining information internally or meditating on these truths.

In addition to this, our technological age has seen historical facts destabilized by films, TV shows and books blurring truth for dramatic effect. 'Based on a true story' does not mean true.[5] Absolute historical fact can be eroded, sometimes to the point of being considered by some to be myth. What more horrific evidence of this do we need in our generation than the emergence of holocaust deniers? Added to this, there is a sense from some members of society that history itself is not only destabilized, but downgraded and devalued in this new age; things have moved on so much, and newer is always better, so why even go there? Sometimes it can feel like we only revisit history when some controversial historian has attempted to rewrite it, or some newly discovered knowledge claims to reframe the truth we have been told. Maybe each new generation does this part of the circle of rebellion against what has gone before, but the concern is that the past is seen as a solely negative force. Mindfulness expert Jay Shetty seems to suggest this when he says: 'We live in the past with

---

5 Watchers of *The Crown* take note.

nostalgia of "the good old days" as if there is some sort of safety there and we stop ourselves from creating a new world with new memories. Nostalgia makes us feel safe, but it's not safe at all and stops us from living our lives.'ᵛ

Culture of forgetting

So, what does this mean for our spiritual walk? I, for one, love the instant access and accurate information that is available on the internet, but I sometimes wonder if the internet is akin to the tree of the knowledge of good and evil (Gen. 2.9). It seems that though there is so much good on it, the bad stuff just has no bounds. It's just a thought – undoubtedly the internet has enriched our lives in many ways; it's just the impact on spiritual processes in our lives that concerns me.

Don't let the world around you squeeze you into its own mould, but let God re-mould your minds from within, so that you may prove in practice that the plan of God for you is good, meets all his demands and moves towards the goal of true maturity. (Rom. 12.2, PHILLIPS)

The processes, fashions and cultures of the world change over time. Though the methodologies of how we connect with other Christians, read the word and worship may alter over time, God's truth and instructions do not. So the question for us is this: In God's economy, is remembering a methodology or is it truth and instruction?

Our culture is all about the now and the instant, and often it can feel like many Christians and churches have also squeezed into this mould of negating the past. There is rightly a focus on the historical times that we see in Scripture, and that helps us in turn to understand hidden depths in God's word. But for many, that seems to be where the historical interest ends; proportionally speaking, there is little reference to the time between the end of the New

Testament and the present-day Church. At least, as I've travelled the country and beyond to speak to churches, it seems that the countless miracles and numerous adventures of answered prayer seem to be excluded from our daily church life, with often comparatively little attention given to the stories of the founders of each church movement. We talk about standing on the shoulders of giants, but how much time do we take to find out what gave them their strength?

Naturally, God is often 'doing a new thing' (Isa. 43.19) and we don't want to miss that, but it seems to me that we have a myopic focus on what God is doing *now,* glossing over much benefit to be found in the past. And if you think these are sweeping generalizations, here are some questions. How much time has your church spent focusing on what God has done previously rather than now? How much of your teaching programmes capture the stories of faith heroes of the past, ancient or modern? How much opportunity is there for the elderly to pass on stories to the young in the communities you are in? If an answered prayer has eternal value, then why the focus in church meetings on testimonies that have happened that week and only that week? Are we saying to all the senior citizens among us that we don't want to hear what God has done in your past, that it's not relevant and we just want the now? I don't believe that's in anybody's heart, but culture squeezes us that way and by our actions speaks that message. And, particularly, when it comes to our faith, there is a difference between accessing facts, *remembering* facts in our minds and owning these facts in our lives. Take the following three steps, for example:

1 'Where does it say in the Bible, don't worry?' Google says, 'Matthew 6.34'.
2 I remember the scripture 'Therefore do not worry about tomorrow, for tomorrow will worry about itself.'
3 I don't worry about tomorrow.

If we stop at Step 1, we leave the process being informed of God, not *knowing* him. The challenge with an enhanced ability to access facts is that they rarely become truths. The individual knows where to find a scripture on a topic and increasingly becomes adept at locating it, but the fact is not owned, it is not imbibed. They never get to Step 3. I'm thankful for the technology that helps me find the scriptures, but it is my responsibility to ensure that a scripture is learnt, remembered and becomes part of me and the way I live my life. I'm sure the makers of YouVersion Bible App[6] are more focused on helping you to do the latter too. The benefits of meditating on the word in such a way helps us to remember God's deeds, who he is and what he has done. We'll see in later chapters the significant benefits of this in empowering our faith, providing peace for the now and, importantly, how this meditation can have an impact on the future.

In the same way as the technological age is affecting our transactive memory on a personal level, this also applies to our churches where we are encouraged to meet together (Heb. 10.24–25). Groups and households meeting together, sharing the experience of discovering more of God together should not be jettisoned because it's easier to find the Scripture online or listen to some podcast. Our destiny is not called to be a dysfunctional disparate body of people; on the contrary, our joint experience as a church is what makes us strong in our pursuit of him.

It may be that you're reading this knowing that remembering and recalling God's deeds is a regular part of your devotional time, and if that's the case, that's wonderful. But if you're anything like me, it may be that you have been subject to the squeezing of the world's mould in regard to the habit of not remembering or devaluing history more than you are aware. If you're not sure where you fall on this spectrum, here are some questions to help you explore just that:

6 YouVersion is great – despite its highlighting that my 'Read the Bible in a Year 2017' plan remains a work in progress.

1 Can you remember five times in your life when you have prayed and God has answered?
2 When was the last time you sat down and took time to reflect, recall and remember something that God did in your life a few years ago?
3 Of your closest Christian friends, how many stories do you know of the miraculous things God has done in their lives, or their salvation story?
4 To what extent is remembrance part of your regular devotional routine?

There is, of course, no condemnation for those in Christ Jesus (Rom. 8.1), but the questions are there to highlight that largely our Christian experience of remembering is much removed from Old Testament times. What remembrance we do encounter is often centred around the memorizing of Scripture, but not on the personal acts of God in our lives and the lives of others. And yet we see in the next chapter that remembering God's deeds is a practice that is as close to his heart as it is foundational to the building of an intimate relationship with him.

Answered prayer: 21 March 2020

During the Covid-19 crisis, Kendra – based in Nicaragua – prays and asks God to show her a way she can be used at this time. Later that day, she gets a call from a missionary organization asking for her help. They had a colleague who had tried to ship a container of medical equipment to Nicaragua, but this had been beset with many complications and it had got lost, stuck somewhere in the system. They soon sent Kendra the email trail of a story which began in the autumn of 2015.

A man from Colorado had visited Nicaragua, and God had placed on his heart the burden to send medical supplies to that country;

he puts his heart and soul into sharing the vision, raising money and arranging the practicalities to make this happen. Finally, in August 2019, he was able to ship the container, but due to incorrect paperwork, he could not get it out of customs and it fell into abandonment. The founder of this project was stuck in his efforts to release it from customs, and it seemed all his time and the money of his supporters was wasted.

Cue Kendra praying. She goes to the customs office to find out what's happened and is told that the container was sent away for auction because it was abandoned. Kendra, invested in God's commission, doesn't take no for an answer and asks to see the paperwork – due to an administrative error, they find it hasn't actually left the warehouse. 'Can you try and locate it?' Kendra asks, her heart full of hope. And they do. And it's *full* of personal protective medical equipment, ventilators, oxygen and more. It's like someone has prepared this package perfectly for what they need to tackle the coronavirus. Kendra is able to get the container released, and the supplies serve 19 hospitals in Nicaragua. God put a burden in someone's heart in 2015, this person was obedient and nearly five years later, in God's perfect timing, it is fulfilled for his Glory.

Practical steps

1 Read through this answered prayer above. Imagine or discuss with friends what it would have been like to be the man from Colorado with the original vision. What does this teach you about what God is like?

2 Why not get yourself a cuppa and a blank piece of paper and give yourself 15 minutes to begin to think what God has done in your life. Just write down the headlines and put it aside to review later on in the book.

3 Spend some time specifically thanking God for the things you can remember.

2
Why is the Bible on repeat?

If I have seen further
it is by standing on the
shoulders of giants.
(Isaac Newton)

If you ask the Jewish people in the present day for a story that defined them, I imagine many would tell you it was God's deliverance of his people from Egypt, as told in the book of Exodus. The story is repeated over and over again in the Bible and in their traditions. The story of how God rescued his people from Pharaoh, the parting of the sea and the pillar of fire that led them to freedom is so ingrained in Jewish culture that it has become part of their identity. And not only the story but the message within it: that they are God's special people. Within Scripture, the Exodus story is repeated immediately after its initial telling, recalled in psalms and referenced in the Old Testament by prophets and in New Testament letters. So why is the Bible on repeat?

Is God obsessed with remembering?

When I started my journey of collecting answered prayers, I expected that God would teach me more about prayer, but it was the thematic strand of remembrance which flows through the word of God that I felt he was speaking to me about most. I went through one of those stages where everything you read, listen to and watch all seems to be pointing towards the topic God is speaking to you about. Above and beyond the prompts around me, I could suddenly see the topic of remembrance was undeniably everywhere in his word. Remembering is referenced in 50 of the 66 books of the Bible, and there are over one thousand scriptures that directly address the subject matter without even covering the prophetic and physical triggers that point to it. Clearly, the power and poignancy of remembrance is very much on God's agenda.

How many repetitions to communicate?

When I first became a Christian and bought my first Bible, I started to get really frustrated by the amount of times a story is repeated or referenced. I felt there were more repeats in the word of God than on BBC One on a Friday night. I was half tempted to take my Bible back to the bookstore and get a refund: 'There's a lot of repetition in this, mate!' Taking the Exodus story alone, we see over 167 times in the Bible where it is in some way revisited. The phrase 'brought you out of Egypt' itself is repeated 32 times alone. And this repetition is not exclusive to Exodus; the life of Jesus is recorded in four gospels, all covering the same story from four different perspectives, for example. Scriptures are repeated and referenced in succeeding books and letters. I struggle to believe that our creator God, who has formed billions of stars and masterminded the creation of millions of species, sort of ran out of content when it came to writing a book.[1] So why is the Bible so full of retelling and recounting its stories?

One could argue that the reason that there is so much repetition in the Bible is that it is God's communication strategy. Research over the last century has varied in its view of how many times a message needs to be communicated before it is retained by the hearer. The clever marketing term is 'effective frequency', and it varies between three and 20. From personal experience, I can tell you that my wife has discovered the optimum level is five. This is partly influenced by the fact that by the fifth time she says 'Have you put the bins out?' the tone has changed somewhat, which tends to cause not only retention but also immediate action. This communicative repetition is seen multiple times with multiple messages. The proclamation 'You will be my people, and I will be your God' has a high level of repetition in different forms in the Old Testament. It's way over the marketing three-to-20 level, though, to be fair, God may argue that two thousand years later we still haven't got the hang of it, so the repeats are not misplaced.

---

1 A similar line of thought also takes me to consider why the God of infinite creativity struggles to make a 40-minute preach interesting, though I rather suspect on occasion he has less influence in this area than most of the listeners would like.

It doesn't stop there. The book of Kings, for example, has over 20 references to shrines being built or unremoved in the high places. From 'Although he did not remove the high places' (1 Kgs 15.14) to 'The high places, however, were not removed' (1 Kgs 22.43), the repetition in part is perhaps to add extra emphasis. But when we see the same modus operandi attributed to God's deeds in Scripture, it's more than just a highlighting technique. I'm uncomfortable with the thought that God is using some sort of nagging approach to enable us to retain important information, or some marketing effective frequency – that doesn't sit right.[2] But so prevalent is the theme of remembering that it cannot be ignored. Not only does God encourage us to remember, he sets the example.

Remembering in the Bible

The first reference in the Scriptures regarding remembrance is, of course, the rainbow. God creates an external symbol to prompt memory. Whereas elsewhere in the Scriptures the creation of a physical trigger is there to remind the individual of what God had done, in this case, the physical trigger is for God himself: 'Whenever I bring clouds over the earth and the rainbow appears in the clouds, I will remember my covenant between me and you and all living creatures of every kind' (Gen. 9.14–15).

After the story of Noah, there are countless prompts and calls to remember what God has done. Beginning with Jacob in Genesis laying a stone to recall his encounter with God at Bethel (Gen. 28.18) and repeated multiple times, up to 1 Samuel (7.7–12), where Samuel lays a stone to remember God's help, we see the laying of

---

2 It also contradicts the husband's favourite scripture to be pulled out of a hat when losing an argument: 'Better to live in a desert than with a quarrelsome and nagging wife.' (Proverbs 21.19) To be honest, can't say it's ever helped me win any argument with my better half, and in my opinion and experience, is best avoided, chaps.

stones to remember an encounter with God or a God-given victory. In Old Testament times, a shepherd would mark his staff to remember God's deeds, and this prophetic picture allows further insight into remembering from Genesis to Psalms. Multiple times we read the psalmists recounting the deeds of God. Then we see Jesus teaching the disciples about the power of remembrance, and remembering him is stipulated as an essential element of the covenant meal. Lastly, in the book of Revelation, the power of remembering the stories of Jesus is revealed as a way to overcome the challenges of life: 'They triumphed over him, by the blood of the Lamb and by the word of their testimony' (Rev. 12.11a). From beginning to end of the Bible, we see evidence after evidence that God is passionate about the topic of remembering; he is consistently encouraging us to remember, and we even see stark warnings for those who choose not to. In the following chapters, we will investigate the Scriptures to see what it is that we should be remembering and how, in broad brushstrokes, remembering undergirds the deepening of our relationship with God, strengthening the foundations of our love for him and our understanding of his love for us in return. As with most spiritual truths, this is best explained by a Hollywood rom-com.[3]

It's all about the story

It was on one of our regular film nights that my wife and I decided (well, really I was persuaded) to watch a rom-com called *Fifty First Dates*. You may have seen the movie yourself, but, in short, the set-up is this: Drew Barrymore, starring as the female lead, has short-term memory loss, and one day she meets Adam Sandler, her male co-star. They connect and have a great first date. The following day, she meets him again, but this time with no recollection of their first date

---

3 For those who are worried, I *am* joking, but humour me . . .

– or even who he is. Once Sandler's character learns of Barrymore's character's memory loss, he vows to win her love over the following 49 first dates. It's an okay film – the 6.8 rating on IMDB says it all. I know the scriptwriters intended this movie to be a light-hearted comedy, but watching it, I felt a weight of sadness that the characters could never really have any depth of relationship with each other. Spoiler alert: they marry at the end, and each day has to begin with her watching a video explanation by her husband to get her up to speed with who he is. Despite this cute way the characters find to enable them to live a happy life together, in reality (if this were reality) she would always be playing catch up and moving forward in relationship with him on limited details and shallow foundations. Inevitably, much of the intimacies and intricacies we learn of each other in a long-term relationship are not there in this film – forgetfulness prevents their love going deeper. This, I believe, is not God's intention for the bride of Christ; in fact, it is the complete antithesis of the *Fifty First Dates* premise. Instead, God is always looking to deepen our relationship with him, and we do so through remembering.

If we step back to take a look at the broad story of Scripture, it is one where God is constantly calling us, his Church – the Bride of Christ – ever closer to him. Through the passing of time, we learn in increasing measure of his love for us, until in the end, in perfect understanding we are joined with Christ for eternity. The story is not smooth; there are times when we forget and stumble and times when we have to retrace our steps before we can move forward, but ultimately, if we are walking in step with the Holy Spirit, we grow in our understanding of Jesus's love for us until it's perfected in eternity. And, of course, the only way we can do this while we're on the journey is by remembering what's already happened and by considering the experiences and knowledge of the heroes of the faith who have gone before us. This is why I believe God places such heavy emphasis on remembering – because it's all about building and deepening our relationship with him. That is why the word encourages us to listen to the generations before us and pass our story on to the generation behind, so that each generation that begins their journey in following God does not have to go through Drew Barrymore's repeated experience of discovering who her first love is. As Deuteronomy 32.7 encourages us: 'Remember the days of old; consider the generations long past.'

Through time, and generation after generation, God reveals himself through stories. Stories of betrayal reveal his redemption, stories of need reveal his provision, stories of weakness reveal his strength, and so on. It's not a coincidence that Jesus's communication to us in the New Testament was not through difficult-to-grasp theology but by appealing to our hearts through stories. Every story told reveals another layer of his relationship with us, and if we remember each one, we can learn more.

We can see, therefore, that the reason the Bible is full of encouragement to recount and retell is that these practices encourage progression, rather than repetition, in our relationship with God. Every old memory reveals a new depth to his nature. When we forget the learning in an experience, it has to either be relived so that the learning is restored, or the past stories need to be found and remembered so that we can build and build on who we know God is.

Answered prayer: 1980s

This story is told anonymously from a trusted source.

Kabul was under curfew at the time, and tensions were high. On my second night in the city, after dark, about 10 p.m., I had to make my way to a rendezvous with my contact. Things didn't go well, as we were spotted by the police, who set off the alarms and gave chase. Jumping on the motorcycle (with me driving), we dashed through the darkened streets, and my contact jumped off and ran into the shadows. I had to continue on with no map and no knowledge of where I was going. There was some shooting, and more military vehicles were coming out, blocking intersections and giving chase. Once I stopped at a place where I became boxed in, military trucks and jeeps in front and behind me. As the soldiers dismounted from their vehicles, I felt God's prompting to seize the moment and race away again. My heart was pounding. I just rode northwards, and then westwards – I kept going into the hills. I stopped on the roadside after an hour or so; no one was chasing, and it was still and quiet. I had no documents, no address of the safe house, a little money and a lot of fear. *Should I keep going and try to get through one of the borders to the north? Or should I turn around and go back into Kabul, despite not knowing my way to the safe house?* I prayed. I cried out to God for his intervention, his prompting. He said clearly that I should return to Kabul and that he would guide me and protect me. I went back down the hill roads, towards the city.

Dawn was coming; the half-light was drawing more people out into the streets that had been deserted a few hours before. Approaching every junction, I would pray: 'Which way, God?' If I didn't get a left or right prompting, I would carry straight on. I saw police, I saw the military, but the streets were increasingly full of the traffic of the day, and no one paid any attention to me. I drove carefully, with the flow of the traffic, all the time in conversation with God: 'Which way now?' 'Please keep me hidden from their view, under your wings.' I think the journey took me two to three hours. I never stopped. I never retraced my steps or made a U-turn. I have no idea what route I took. But I arrived in the crowded courtyard in the outskirts of a suburb at the gated door to the safe house. Only God can do this.

Practical steps

1 With a group of friends, or perhaps a WhatsApp group if you want to engage in this remotely, see how many books of the Bible you can find that refer to remembrance in its scriptures.
2 Search the Scriptures for those that contain the word 'remember' – what do you find?
3 In your quiet time with God, reflect on how highly he values remembrance. Are your values aligned with God's?

3
The forgotten giver

You have forgotten God your Saviour; you have not remembered the Rock, your fortress. (Isa. 17.10)

When my son James was a little boy, our approach to potty training was to reward him with a point every time he had a – well, let's just say a 'successful excursion'! It was your classic parental reward system. Every time he was able to run upstairs to the potty before any mishaps, either my wife Sarah or I would check on the evidence before giving him a sticker which he then proudly put on his chart that we had hung up on the wall. Once he amassed enough points, he would get a present: *Well done, son, five poos to go!* For the record, the cost of said present was easily offset by the savings in nappies and cleaning products.

Soon the day came when the last no. 2 arrived, which meant the week's chart was complete and the present-purchasing was imminent. And so, we would jump in the car and speed off to the toy shop just a couple of miles from home. Amid the prams, buggies and various other 'essential' baby and child paraphernalia, there was a small area for Thomas the Tank Engine wooden engine sets; other wooden engine sets were available, but not as good – or at least that's what he told me. The first time we arrived, James spent ages choosing which of these wooden engines to select, picking one up and putting it back, over and over. It was just too much for him to take in, an overload of opportunity. Eventually, he settled on the 'right' one. With 'Thank you, Daddy,' he'd fling his arms around me, and we would rush back to ours. As soon as we got home, James would open his toy with great excitement, lay out all his track, put out all his existing trains in a specific order and then, with tremendous precision, add his new acquisition to the mix, perfectly in line with the other trains. He'd play for a while, enjoying the fruits of his labour, arranging and rearranging the trains with glee and gratitude.

After a while, the 'nappies for trains' programme was working beautifully, and we were starting to get into a new rhythm. After each efficient toilet trip, James would put a sticker on his chart and eagerly await our toy shop adventure. Now knowing what to expect, he'd get so worked up on the journey there that it felt like he would explode with all the pent-up energy; he'd spend the whole car ride talking about the different engines he thought he was going to buy, his mind running fast with all the possibilities, his mouth running even faster. When we would get to the shop, he'd run round to the section that sold the engines and, without hesitation, grab the one that he wanted before sprinting to the till and rushing us home to play.

Then an interesting thing happened. Before long, James went back to the packaging of his chosen engine, took out the small folded catalogue and started to decide which one he would get next. We started to notice that he began to spend more time pondering his next reward than he did on enjoying the rewards he had already received. Conversations at teatime were filled with his angst and deliberations about which one he should have next.

Over the course of a few weeks, the amount of time he played with the engines decreased, and the amount of time spent poring over the catalogue increased. Then the final day of 'trains for poos' came: into the shop, engine grabbed, straight to the till, no pleases, no thank you, no loving embraces. We rushed home and James ran into the lounge, ripping open the train box. The engine he had bought fell out of the box and fell to one side, completely ignored. Instead, he went straight to the leaflet to decide what his next request was going to be. The 'nappies for engines' campaign was brought to an abrupt halt. Enough was enough – James loved the excitement, the anticipation, the process, but in it all, not only had he promptly dismissed the gift, but, more importantly, he had also forgotten the giver. Our generosity towards him had been overshadowed by the excitement of what was coming next, and he'd started to take the gifts – and our generosity – for granted. I was cross with James's attitude. And as has happened so many times in my life when I begin to judge the actions of others, elevating myself above them, I hear the familiar voice of the Holy Spirit whispering, 'You do that too.'

How do we forget God?

In simple terms, forgetting what God has done is like carrying a picture of him around to remember what he looks like, then losing it and not even realizing that you ever had it. It may seem at first incongruous that we could possibly completely erase God's mighty deeds from our senses, but as Ogawa says in *The Memory Police*, 'People—and I'm no exception—seem capable of forgetting almost anything.' And not just people individually, but collectively. The Bible makes clear that we are to remember together: 'Only be careful, and watch yourselves closely so that you do not forget the things your eyes have seen or let them fade from your heart as long as you live. Teach them to your children and to their children after them' (Deut. 4.9). And yet in many ways, as we will explore in the remainder of this chapter, the nation of the UK has corporately forgotten God answering.

Though the importance of remembering personally and corporately is clear, King Solomon also identifies that part of our sinful nature is to forget: 'no one remembers the former generations' (Eccl. 1.11), with Deuteronomy adding weight to the dangers of this spiritual amnesia with over 15 verses warning us to work against this tendency to forget. Above and beyond our own sinful nature, perhaps it is an enemy strategy to ensure we don't grow in our knowledge of God but keep returning time after time to a blank canvas.

Forgetfulness leads to a loss of thankfulness

If when God acts, he reveals who he is, then the Devil will surely want us to forget that as soon as possible. He may do that by causing confusion at the moment of God's intervention – *did it really happen?* – or the miraculous outcome may be attributed to human effort or coincidence. The poet Lord Tennyson is attributed with saying: 'When I pray, coincidences happen, and when I don't pray, they don't,' and yet we can all too easily celebrate God's goodness in the moment of answered prayer and, within days, start to explain the outcomes away as fortuitous happenings. Arguably, distraction is the most commonly used device to deflect us from God at work. The enemy strategy is pretty simple: the more God's deeds are forgotten, the more the revelation of him is diminished in a generation. If the battle of God acting is wrought in prayer, then the war is won or lost in its remembering. Central to our faith is the attitude of thankfulness; as we thank God, we remember who he is, transporting us into a place of worship. That's why the psalmist instructs us to 'enter his gates with thanksgiving and his courts with praise; give thanks to him and praise his name' (Ps. 100.4). As the iconic writer C. S. Lewis says: 'Gratitude looks to the Past and love to the Present; fear, avarice, lust, and ambition look ahead.'

The media is littered with examples of prayers asked and answered, with the giver left without his due thanks. One example of these occurred in a year I imagine none of us will forget in a hurry. In 2020, the nation was gripped with fear amid the coronavirus crisis, and at its height, we heard the news that Prime Minister Boris Johnson was ill with Covid-19. Fear was put on steroids, as a number of the government ministers were falling ill – and then came the development that Boris was in intensive care. My WhatsApp feeds were filled with Christians and non-Christians alike calling to 'Pray for Boris', and it even became a headline of *The Sun* newspaper. Though we didn't know at the time, Boris had a 50/50 chance of pulling through, and the *Sunday Times* soon reported that ministers and advisors were encouraged to 'just pray'. Then, Boris pulled through and in a video address broadcast from his home, he thanked the nation, thanked the National Health Service, thanked specific nurses and doctors, but the Almighty didn't get a namecheck. Sadly, this lack of gratitude was mirrored in the Christian WhatsApp groups I was a part of, as everyone moved on to the next controversy or emergency to focus our requests, without a murmur of what God had done.

This is not the first time this has happened, even in recent history. On 17 March 2012, professional footballer Fabrice Mwamba had a heart attack while playing for Bolton Wanderers against Tottenham Hotspur in the FA Cup quarter final and collapsed on the pitch. The players knew instantly something really bad had happened. I have heard that one of the players instantly recognized the gravity of the situation, realizing in that moment that his money, his fame and his career counted for nothing, as none of them could help Fabrice. Instead, he just sat on the pitch and prayed. There, on the same pitch where this player sat praying, Fabrice was defibrillated then rushed to hospital by ambulance. His heart stopped for 78 minutes, but he was resuscitated in hospital and lay in a coma.

What followed was a media storm, and the phrase 'Pray for Muamba' spread like wildfire across the globe. Described as being 'deeply religious',[1] Fabrice is a born-again Christian; his family were by his side and praying for his restoration, along with the club chaplain. *The Sun* newspaper ran the headline 'God is in Control – Praying for Muamba'; the *Daily Star* led with 'In God's Hands'. Football players across the world wore 'Pray 4 Muamba' T-shirts, and in the middle of games, celebrating strikers would reveal these under their club shirts and point to the skies. And then he recovered. Miraculously. To live a full life. And how did the media celebrate? They congratulated the bravery and expertise of the medical staff, but the God in whom so many had invested their hope was forgotten. The world bowed down and worshipped at the altar of medical science without noticing God's ability to work through it. I have heard Fabrice tell this story giving all the glory to God, but on a national level, it appeared that, once again, many had called on the God who answers, and faithfully he did, but the giver has been forgotten, faded out of the narrative.

This forgetfulness is not limited to the nation's media and is sadly prevalent among many Christians, directly affecting their ability to worship and show gratitude to the Lord Most High. I have met some

Christians who find it difficult to give thanks and enter into times of praise, as they simply cannot remember a time when God has answered a prayer for them. The first time I heard this, I was staggered. Here was a young junior doctor, standing at the front of church, tearfully telling me how God had never answered a prayer for her. Privately, I wondered why she would bother coming to church to engage with a God who never answers.[1] But as I took the time to talk to this young woman and listened to her life, an interesting thing happened. Sensitively, I asked her what things she had prayed for in the past. I asked how she prayed for them, and then I asked her what happened. She recalled her experiences, her journey, the challenges of university life and the pressures of being a junior doctor. Piece by piece, she was able to remember the things she had called on God for, and then she started to see that in fact he had answered every cry her heart had uttered – she had just never taken the time to really think about it. It was an amazing thing to witness; somehow the pressures of life, the speed of circumstances and continual demand on her time had prevented her from recognizing what had happened along the way. Forgetting God's work in her life had caused her despair and discouragement as she thought God had forgotten her, but the simple act of remembering brought joy and hope.

Forgetfulness leads to taking God for granted

The story of Exodus has many incredible elements, but it also highlights the astounding forgetfulness of the Israelites and its power to distract us from the truth. Dramatically delivered from oppression, experiencing first-hand the power of the Almighty, taking part in one of the most amazing stories ever told – and within days of being rescued from oppression, the Israelites begin having a moan about

---

1 Once again, my pastoral gift shining through.

food: 'In the desert, the whole community grumbled against Moses and Aaron' (Exod. 16.2). So with incredible grace, God provides quail in the morning and manna in the evening to sustain them. Again, after only a few days, they are complaining again, this time about the water. Are you kidding me? But before I get too judgy about perceiving prayer as nothing more than a shopping list with which to approach some sort of supermarket God, I know in my heart that I have done the same to my Father in heaven – he has become my forgotten giver.

I don't know about you, but I find this cycle of new needs such an easy trap to fall into. For a time my attention is focused on a specific need, a defined want which I present to God in prayer. In that moment, it's all I think about. *If only* . . . If only God would answer, if only that healing would come, if only that finance would arrive, if only that change of attitude, if only that job opportunity, if only that salvation of a friend, if only that miracle of a change in circumstances. And when Jesus clearly answers, it is a moment of such elation, such thrill, such euphoria that I experience that intimate connection with the God of all creation. Then before long, the days and weeks pass, sometimes even less than that, and I'm on to the next thing, on to the next prayer request. The emotional strength has gone, the confidence has dissipated and I'm pleading again to the God who answers, forgetting all the while that he already has. How can I let that happen?

Forgetfulness leads to fear

I'm not the first human being who has travelled from moments of faith to ones of fear and forgetfulness in a short space of time. We see the same in the word of God. In 1 Kings 18, Elijah does an incredible thing – he stands in front of a hostile band of prophets on Mount Carmel and declares for the one true God. Then we read the incredible miracle of how he calls on God to set fire to the sacrifice on the altar he has built. Elijah stood there before them all and even had the audacity to pour water on the wood to make it more difficult for God to show his glory – which of course, he does. This is some faith, incredible confidence and assurance in the God who answers. Then, as Elijah calls on him, the fire comes down and burns wood, sacrifice, stone and every last drop of water. Just imagine yourself in Elijah's shoes; you have got to be pumped, right? Does any miracle of God get more awesome than when your very life is on the line, you call for fire and he answers? And yet . . .

Only days later (1 Kgs 19.4), we find Elijah hiding under a bush, fearing for his life and wanting to die; he has had enough. He has moved from assurance in God to doubt, travelled from joy to despair and fallen into a deep depression. This is some negative transformation – so what happened? After the Carmel fire, we see another miracle, this time one of rain, but Queen Jezebel gets wind of his action and sends a messenger to deliver a threat to Elijah's life: 'May the gods deal with me, be it ever so severely, if by this time tomorrow I do not make your life like that of one of them' (1 Kgs 19.2). And in that instant, fear comes into him and dominates. Understandably, the threat on his life diminishes the faith that has preceded and increases the fear. The intensity of emotion is like a magnifying glass, focusing in on all that is wrong, and God's miracles seem a distant memory from a disconnected past. It's somewhat ironic that Elijah's accusation to the Carmel prophets of wavering between two opinions (God and Baal) (1 Kgs 18.21) is in effect exactly what he is doing now – oscillating between faith and fear. I find it comforting to know it's not just me! Elijah has moved from full of faith to full of fear, extreme life-threatening anxiety. I believe he forgot to remember. Not just to recall the miracle on Mount Carmel, but to remember who God was in that moment and remember that as he was, he is. God never changes; the God who performed those miracles in Elijah's day is the God who hears our prayers today. Forgetting can not only lead to a pathway of fear, anxiety and depression, but conversely also an overconfidence in our ability.

Forgetfulness leads to pride

In the Bible, we see another result of forgetting to remember what God has done: pride. Deuteronomy 8.10–14 reads:

> Be careful that you do not forget the LORD your God . . . Otherwise, when you eat and are satisfied, when you build fine houses and settle down, and when your herds and flocks grow large and your silver and gold increase and all you have is multiplied, then your heart will become proud and you will forget the LORD your God, who brought you out of Egypt, out of the land of slavery.

We can see this playing out in relatively recent history in the miracle of Dunkirk. It is a story that has so captured the UK's heart that embodying the Dunkirk spirit is synonymous with bravery and courage. And yet, though it is part of our national DNA, the truth of what God did has been erased and replaced with national, wholly human pride.

Some of you will know the following story well, but I urge you to renew your focus on God's starring role in the following series of events. After Germany invaded Poland in 1939, the British army moved to support France in defending its border with Belgium. Ten divisions of Britain's expeditionary force were in place to repel any German attack and represented a large percentage of all the country's ground-based troops. In truth, generals and strategists were expecting a First World War-type battle, slow and attritional, but Germany caught them off guard.

On 10 May 1940, Germany attacked both Belgium and Holland. The British-French allies believed that this advance consisted of

Germany's elite forces and pushed into Belgium to confront the attack, but it was a mistake. A surprise attack further south by the cream of Germany's troops smashed through the Ardennes Forest and the French lines, an area that was poorly defended as it was believed to be impenetrable. The Germans proved this belief wrong; employing their blitzkrieg approach of a concentration of tanks attacking at speed, they advanced to the northwest of France in a matter of days. This penetrating attack outflanked the expeditionary forces. The British army was thus surrounded and cut off from the French forces in the south, and realizing the gravity of the situation, Viscount Gort ordered their retreat to Dunkirk. The Germans seemed invincible, and the British troops were psychologically damaged – and, along with some French and Canadian troops, were surrounded and were pushed into a shrinking enclave onto the beaches. The British army was in retreat, the German high command boasting, 'The British army is encircled and our troops are proceeding to its annihilation.' The next part of the story wasn't covered in Christopher Nolan's award-winning film.

On 24 May 1940, His Majesty King George VI announced a National Day of Prayer. In a radio broadcast to the nation, he announced, 'At this fateful hour we turn, as our fathers before us have turned in times of trial, to God Most High. Here in the whole country I have asked that Sunday next will be observed as a day of national prayer . . . and with God's help we shall not fail.'

Later that day, Hitler overruled his generals and halted the advance when only ten miles from Dunkirk. Though his reasons are still not clear, Churchill felt that he did so in the knowledge that annihilation of the British troops was inevitable regardless of timescale, such was the dominance of the German air force. Perhaps it was Hitler's overconfidence in imminent victory that caused a temporary halt, but from a historical perspective, no certainty can be attributed to his decision-making process that day. In hindsight, his decision to exercise his own authority over that of his key advisors is seen as one of the greatest blunders in military history. No one knows exactly why he did it, but what is certain is that the delay gave British troops a window of opportunity to escape. On 26 May, the UK responded in prayer. I've spoken with senior citizens who told me how, as children, they heard the king's call to prayer huddled around a radio, and how they went to church to pray with their mothers. The response to this trumpet call to pray was unprecedented, photographs from the time showing winding queues outside Westminster Cathedral as hundreds waited to offer their prayers to the Lord Most High. It's recorded that over a million people prayed in churches that day. The nation was on its knees, and God answered.

The seas on Dunkirk beach were shallow, meaning that navy ships could not access them. Churchill had been advised that only 30,000 troops could be expected to be saved from the Dunkirk beaches, resulting in an undoubtedly fatal blow for the British army of over 400,000 men lost. However, on 28 May, a storm broke out over Flanders which grounded much of the German Luftwaffe, and Operation Dynamo, the evacuation of Dunkirk, began. This was a miracle of timing, as were the starkly different weather conditions – the fierceness of the storm in Flanders restricting the German air force, contrasting with the calmness of the sea in Dunkirk just a hundred kilometres away. 'The English Channel became as smooth as glass . . . and anything that could float . . . moved across the English Channel under cover of dense fog.'[11] Meanwhile, back in the UK, a fleet of over eight hundred boats had been hastily assembled. The smaller vessels overcame the problem of the shallow seas, and the unusual weather conditions allowed this flotilla to coordinate with the navy to rescue the soldiers from the beaches, largely unhindered by air raids. Just the smallest change in the weather, a marginal change in wind speed, for example, and the evacuation would not have been possible. Coincidence? Even those German planes that did manage to get off the ground created more opportunity for God's goodness to be seen.

The Trumpet Sounds for Britain[III] gives the account of an army chaplain who was on the beach at the time. As a plane came in to attack, he fell to the sand, lying prostrate as fire from the plane's machine gun rained down on him for what seemed like an age. When silence returned, he stood up, amazed that he hadn't been hit, and as he looked down at where he had lain, saw that his body had been silhouetted by bullet marks in the sand. Not a single bullet had touched him.

The evacuation began on the day the nation prayed, 26 May 1940, and continued until 4 June. In all, over 338,226 soldiers were rescued in that time. The Bishop of Chelmsford, Henry Wilson, wrote, 'If ever a great nation was on the point of supreme and final disaster, and yet was saved and reinstated . . . it does not require a religious mind to detect in all this the hand of God.' Though many historians, filmmakers and writers will reflect on the bravery and human courage displayed, even Churchill himself reflected in his memoirs that 'I sometimes have a feeling of interference. I want to stress that. I have a feeling sometimes that some guiding hand has interfered. I have a feeling that we have a guardian because we have a great cause and we shall have that guardian so long as we serve that cause faithfully.'[IV] We know that guardian's name. To the nation's credit, on 9 June 1940, millions met in churches across the UK to give thanks to God in a national day of thanksgiving. For those who now retrospectively dispute God at work at this time, please note the nation was in no doubt; they gave thanks.

And yet, over eighty years later, the divine aspects of this miracle of Dunkirk are largely forgotten, drifting from the national consciousness. In Nolan's film, Hitler's decision to halt the advance is not included. The calmness of the weather on the beaches was jettisoned, with the tougher conditions adding more drama. The fog that covered the boats, that protected those on the beach from the Luftwaffe, is ignored. In fact, more German planes were introduced into the film to create a climax as they fought for dominance in the skies. This cinematic masterpiece highlights the bravery of ordinary men and women, young and old, who crossed into the arena of war, a sacrifice that none of us should ever forget. But it makes no mention of a king calling the nation to pray for only the fifteenth time in history. It makes no mention of the multitudes who, in their time of great trial, decided to turn to the God who answers. The truth has been confiscated by the film industry intent on only stirring emotions and tickling ears. In an age when history is often redefined by populist media, one of the greatest miracles we have seen on these isles has been subtly erased from our memory and thus lost for the generations that follow. We have to defend the truth; we have to tell our children and our children's children.

The way that the story of Dunkirk is recounted is perhaps again indicative of the enemy's strategy when it comes to the things of God. When God blesses us with an answered prayer, there is almost always an immediate challenge to its validity and hence the need for consolidation, which we'll explore more later in this book. It is all too easy to forget God in giving man the glory. As John Priestly[V] puts it, 'And our great-great-grand-children, when they learn how we began this war by snatching glory out of defeat, and then swept on to victory, may also learn how the little holiday steamers made an excursion to hell and came back glorious.'

I in no way want to undermine the boldness and bravery of those fishermen and holiday steamer captains – they should be honoured – but it is a dangerous thing to decide not to recognize God's part in the story. Who gave those fishermen courage? Who put the fog in place? Who calmed the storm in one place and yet fueled it in another? Who changed the minds of leaders? Let's ensure that when our great-great-grandchildren learn how we began this war by snatching glory out of defeat, they learn we did so not only by the bravery of soldiers or the courage of fishermen, but by the faithfulness of a nation to call on the Lord Most High in a time of trouble and by the faithfulness of that Lord Most High to answer.

And this is just one story where truth seems to have been eradicated. If you're prepared to look hard enough and dig deep enough, you will find the work of God's hand behind the scenes of every page of history. Over the years, I have loved taking a second look at the history that I learned as a teenager, finding out decades later that God was in it. As one who obsessed over American politics, for example, it was fascinating to find out that amid all the turmoil caused by the Watergate scandal, God was working on Nixon's 'Hatchet Man' Chuck Colson, who gave his life to Christ. From being one of the most feared men in the White House, jailed for his misdemeanours, he founded the Prison Fellowship and authored thirty Christian books. And then sometimes we see answers to prayer in plain sight, like Dunkirk, and still the media are able to cover it up, to allow the truth to fade.

The consequence of forgetting such things is we get puffed up on our own ability to overcome adversity, creating an independence which is an affront to God. It's a dangerous state when we all know what pride comes before. For many, the dangers lie not in temptation, not in distraction, but in success. It's when we are surrounded by an environment of things going well that it can lead us to forget the God who answered our cries. Forgetting in the plenty has consequences; it causes a proud heart, and it can cause destruction. As Deuteronomy 8.19 warns: 'If you ever forget the LORD your God . . . I testify against you today that you will surely be destroyed.' Remembering keeps us humble.

There are times in my own journey when there is much backslapping, congratulations and admiration around what my friends and I have been able to achieve, and though I recognize the importance of honouring each other in our adventures for God, when on the receiving end of so much praise, it can be all too easy to take too much of the credit. If I'm honest, I wouldn't have had a cat in hell's chance of getting past even the first hurdles in life without God's help.[2] I'm

---

2 My university friend Dave at my wedding helpfully pointed out to my parents how pleased he was I had 'seen the light'. 'I'm pretty sure Richie would have drunk himself to death by now were it not for God.' Thanks for that, Dave; your timing is slightly off, but you speak wise words.

ashamed of the times that I have turned my back and forgotten our heavenly giver, where success has tempted me to reflect on my own abilities rather than remembering that it is he who has built the foundation of my life. It is important for us all to remember his hand on our life, the Jesus stories that have brought us to this place where we currently reside.

Answered prayer: late 1800s

A prominent minister in Canada relates the following remarkable instance of God's miraculous care over his people.

Some time ago, on a stormy night, I was suddenly impressed to go to the distant house of an aged couple, and there to pray. So imperative was the call that I harnessed the horse and drove to the spot, fastened the horse under the shed and entered the house unperceived, by a door which had been left open. There, kneeling down, I poured out my petitions to God, in an audible voice, for divine protection over the inmates, after which I departed and returned home. Months after, I was visiting one of the principal prisons in Canada, and moving among the prisoners, was accosted by one of them, who claimed to know me. I had no recollection of the convict and was fairly startled when the latter said: 'Do you remember going to such a house one night and offering prayer in the dark for the inmates?' I told him I did and asked how he came to know anything about it. He said: 'I had gone to that house to steal a sum of money, known to be in the possession of the old man. When you drove into the yard, I thought you were he and intended to kill you while you were hitching your horses. I saw when you spoke to the horse you were a stranger. I followed you into the house and heard your prayer. You prayed to God to protect the old people from violence of any kind, and especially from murder; and if there was any hand uplifted to strike them, that it might be paralyzed.' Then the prisoner pointed to his right arm, which hung lifeless by his side, saying: 'Do you see that arm? It was paralyzed on the spot, and I have never moved it since. Of course, I left the place without doing any harm.'[i]

Practical steps

1 Take some time to reflect on your life and walk with God. Consider if there are any stories where you have forgotten to thank him.
2 Write them down, and as you do, thank God for them.
3 Tell a friend a story you have remembered.

Part 2

WHAT TO REMEMBER

4

Disposable trinkets
or eternal gifts?

So do not throw away your confidence; it will be richly rewarded. (Heb. 10.35)

I believe that understanding God's answered prayer in our lives has weighty ramifications, not only for ourselves but in the lives of others. In the following chapters, I will demonstrate that a continuing and developing knowledge of what God has done in our life stories and in the life stories of others leads not only to a personal spiritual revolution but creates an atmosphere for revival. But before we go there, it's important to consider what constitutes an 'answered prayer'.

As I have talked on the subject of 'answered prayer' and shared stories of God's mighty deeds, I have often done so to a silent congregation. I'm not sure if you've ever spoken publicly to a largely unresponsive room, but it's quite disconcerting. *Why is no one responding? Am I just preaching rubbish today? Again.* The insecurities can race through your mind – or at least, they do for me. I have learnt over the years that such silence does not mean resistance. Often people are processing and comparing such wonderful stories to their own experience. In these quiet environments, more often than not there were people who were overwhelmed with the struggle of their own 'unanswered' prayers; they had often experienced the pain of losing a loved one, or after many years had not seen a breakthrough in a matter close to their heart. I remember one lady saying, 'I would swap everything in the world just to have had that one prayer answered.' The noise of 'unanswered' prayers in the heart of the believer was so loud that it drowned out all else, to the point where no other accounts could be heard without going through the filter of disappointment and hurt. I don't think there is a Christian on the planet who hasn't asked God the question 'Why haven't you answered?' or 'Why have you answered for them and not for me?'

Not one answer

Sometimes, in our hurt and pain in waiting for 'answered prayers', it's easy to miss the fact we are often waiting for God to answer our prayers in the way *we* want him to. There are, of course, many ways that God can answer prayer. In fact, I do not personally believe in the concept of unanswered prayer for his followers at all. Sure, there are times when we feel that God is not responding, and we can empathize with the psalmist in his anguish when he says, 'My God, I cry out by day, but you do not answer, by night, but I find no rest' (Ps. 22.1–2), but there is a weight of Scripture to suggest that God listens to every cry. In 1 Peter, it talks about the Lord's eyes being on the righteous and attentive to every cry (3.12) and within that famous scripture Jeremiah 29.11–12, the prophet recalls God's promise to his people: 'I know the plans I have for you.' 1 John 5.14 says, 'This is the confidence we have in approaching God: that if we ask anything according to his will, he hears us.'

Sometimes it seems our prayers are met with silence,[1] but often and, simply put, it is because the answer to our request is sometimes no. If Jesus can pray in the garden of Gethsemane (Matt. 26.39) and be met with a no, then why shouldn't we? Author and church leader Timothy Keller puts it like this: if our God is big enough for us to be angry with when he says no, then is he also big enough to be wiser than we are? There are countless answered prayers in my life where God has said no, and as time has trickled by, I can now look back and give thanks for that answer. There are also many nos which sit on a shelf waiting for understanding, and they always seem to be the most painful ones. They are still answers to prayer, and with them I choose to submit to God's sovereignty, his wisdom and his love.

There are other times where the answer appears *unquantifiable*. For example, if I pray for a car parking space and one materializes, then we may celebrate this as a clear answer to prayer – although, as we've seen in the previous chapter, many of us may still write this off as a coincidence. And yet, there are other things the Bible calls us to ask God for that may be less easy to quantify in practice. What about when we ask for wisdom? In 1 Kings 3 we find God commending Solomon for choosing to pray for wisdom, yet how clearly do we recognize 'wisdom' as a finite answer to prayer rather than a gradual development in our character more into the likeness of Jesus, which can only happen through God's grace? For this reason, our prayers of 'God give me strength,' and 'Lord grant me patience,' and 'Jesus, I need the grace to deal with this,' often go unrecognized and without thanks.[1]

Sometimes we don't recognize God's answer to our prayers as the answer is *not what we expect*. There are many who enthuse about the benefits of praying for specifics, and I've seen some incredible testimonies as a result of that; I once read about someone asking for a specific bicycle in secret, which miraculously arrived on their doorstep the following day. Arguably more common is the experience that God answers but not in the way we expect – but, in his wisdom, the answer is always better than we could dictate for ourselves. What better example than the Jewish nation who prayed for a messiah? They didn't get what they hoped for, but he was the Saviour of the world.

And then there's the matter of timing. Sometimes the answer to our prayers is *immediate*.

My friend Helen, desperate for food, once sat in her lounge and prayed the Lord's Prayer. Halfway through saying, 'Give us this day our daily bread', when the doorbell rang. As she opened the door, there stood a supermarket delivery man saying they had some spare food and did she want any – for *free*. In my experience, these accounts of immediacy are few and far between, and I often wonder whether this is rooted in the fact that God is far more interested in our journeying with him in prayer rather than the answer itself. For this reason, perhaps, many answers to prayer seem to come *after time*. If I'm honest, it's these prayers that give me the right hump; I always want 'it' yesterday, and so submitting to God's perfect timing

---

1 Very difficult to give God the glory when celebrating an answered prayer regarding humility. I have, though, met a few preachers that have given it a try.

can be tough. I heard of a lady who prayed every day for her husband to be saved; it took fifty years, but eventually God said yes. In Isaiah 55.8 we read, 'For my thoughts are not your thoughts, neither are your ways my ways said the LORD. For as the heavens are higher than the earth, so are my ways higher than your ways, and my thoughts than your thoughts.' God's ways are not our ways, but they are *perfect.* And yet, I know from experience that this knowledge sometimes doesn't make the wait any easier.

Waiting for an answered prayer of healing

When I was 12 years old, I started to experience pains in my lower spine and had some real difficulties with my stomach. I was doing a lot of running at the time and so the doctor presumed it was something to do with pre-race nerves. He prescribed what he thought was appropriate medication – namely, placebos – but the symptoms came and went for a number of years. When I was at university, the pain began to increase in its severity, but once again a trip to the doctor's proved unfruitful. Many years later, having a bad back and dodgy stomach had just become a way of life for me. Working for the church in Cardiff, I had met the love of my life, and we decided to get married. That's when a number of people in the church began expressing concerns about the state of my back linked with my forthcoming marriage.[2] My pastor and good friend Bryan Shutt paid for me to have a private consultation to try and get the symptoms sorted once and for all. The diagnosis was a shock: an incurable disease called ankylosing spondylitis. I was immediately prescribed sixteen tablets a day, but these had very little impact, and if anything, the naming of the disease seemed to give it more power. In layman's terms, the disease causes bone to grow over the cartilage in your spine and has multiple negative effects around inflammation.

---

2   I guess they were worried whether I could carry the luggage on the honeymoon.

Over the coming years, the pain was to get more severe and the disease more debilitating. If anyone has ever been in a healing meeting, you'll know that words of knowledge about bad backs are a common occurrence. I decided, early on, that I would approach each meeting like a child, hoping and praying that God would heal me every time there was such a call. I'd go forward every time and then return back to my seat, disappointed that once again, for whatever reason, I had not been healed. At this point the questions start to fly: *God, why won't you heal me? What am I doing wrong?* To add insult to injury, I then heard of two other people who had been healed of ankylosing spondylitis, and *both* of them are called Richard.

It may be that you've come to this point yourself, but I eventually became sick and tired of people offering to pray for me; I didn't want to deal with the disappointment and failure. By this point I had children, was running a business and planting a church and the pain in my spine had become so severe that I often had to lie down still for two hours a day, sometimes waking in the night, my rib cage in spasm and unable to catch my breath.

Meeting with another GP, I was eventually told that my back is like 'a car in a traffic jam'. 'Mr Gamble,' he went on to explain, 'We can give you medication that will slow down the disease, but at some point the car is going to get to the end of the road. And I'm afraid at that point, you're screwed.' His words, not mine. I left that meeting enraged and made a decision. I was not going to let the word of an expert override the word of God. I started praying, 'Lord, stop the car'.

A few weeks later, I was at a Bible week and as I listened to the preacher, I felt what I can only describe as the presence of God: a tingling, a warmth, a sense that God was there and that he was about to do something. At the end of the sermon, I sprinted to the front for prayer. The preacher asked if he could pour oil down my back, to which I agreed, and as he did, I felt a heat going through my spine – I knew I was healed. I returned to the GP soon after, and an MRI scan revealed that the disease had stopped. The physio that I was sent to looked at my scans and told me how lucky I was; I told her luck had nothing to do with it. What the doctors couldn't do, what medicine couldn't do, God could do. Though it took over 30 years, God in his deep love for me healed me. If you have been asking for an answer over decades, be encouraged he hasn't forgotten; he is still listening.

The treasure from answered prayer

It would be all too easy, after praying for the same thing for so long, to simply thank God and move onto the next, but there is so much treasure to find in any answered prayer that can teach us more of who God is and which can build our faith for the future. From this prayer alone, I can see that

1 Sometimes it takes time to receive an answered prayer. The delay in an answer has no correlation to his love for me.
2 Always approach the throne as a child, choosing to naively believe he can heal today, and not allowing previous disappointments to cloud the truth.
3 God's word is more powerful than that of an expert.
4 Jesus's name is more powerful than the name, diagnosis and definition of ankylosing spondylitis.
5 He shows me similar stories of healing not to test me in jealousy or to mock me, but to show me he can do it, and if he can do it for them, he can do it for me.
6 I need to still contend for my healing, declaring my health when it tries to sneak back.
7 He always has a plan. When I am down and lonely, he has a plan. When I can't see the way forward, he has a plan. He always has a plan.

8 He is faithful even when I am cross and frustrated with him. My
   healing is not dependent on my attitude.
9 Faith comes when you stop wrestling with trying to fathom his
   unfathomable ways.

Is answered prayer a gift?

There is so much treasure to be found in answered prayer that I recently
found myself asking the question: is answered prayer a *gift?* The Bible
instructs us to pray with patience (Rom. 12.12), with persistence
(Col. 4.2), with shameless audacity (Luke 11.8), with confidence
(1 John 5.14–15) and more. And yet, when some propose a system or
framework for 'effective' prayer, I fear at times that doing so presents
our relationship with our heavenly Father as being purely transactional: follow steps A, B, C and D, and this will result in your receiving
an answer. It may seem an attractive guide, but it demotes God to an
answering robot, merely responding to our pressing the right buttons
in the right order. As children of God, the Bible says we have an inheritance, but surely if we act like these answered prayers are our birth-
right, we are at risk of forgetting that when God works in our lives, he
does so without need for recompense – the response is freely given.

For many of us, the first prayer we uttered was one for salvation,
and Jesus responded to our undeserving request: 'for it is by grace
you have been saved' (Eph. 2.8). Eternal life is a gift, through the sacrifice of Jesus on the cross. Our relationship with God, the fact that
we can boldly approach him in prayer, all flows from this gift. Each
divine intervention must be a gracious present, not merely a disposi-
tion nor an obligation to act. Otherwise, we stand dangerously close
to presumption as an ungrateful spoilt child, rather than experiencing the joy of receiving from a generous loving Father. If we see every
answered prayer as a gratuity from heaven rather than a legal right
of inheritance, our response to that answered prayer should be very
different.

In 2 Corinthians 1, the Apostle Paul is reflecting on God's deliverance from the sentence of death in Asia when he says: 'Then many will give thanks on our behalf for the gracious favour granted us in answer to the prayers of many' (v. 11). The phrase Paul uses here is interesting. The Greek word used for 'gracious favour granted' is *charismata*, meaning 'spiritual gift'. Though the term is used elsewhere in the Bible in the context of prophecy, tongues and words of knowledge, here Paul exercises it in relation to answered prayer. Could it be that every time God answers our prayers, it is a spiritual gift from heaven?

If we revisit the age-old question 'Why does God answer some prayers and not others?' in light of this understanding, then perhaps it helps us see that every prayer – answered with a yes, no, not yet or in a way we didn't expect – is God seeking to bless us. As children, we don't always get what we want, and we sometimes ask for the wrong things,[3] things that if God blessed us with at the time would break us. But God doesn't want us broken; he wants us whole in him. As James 1.17 assures us: 'Every good and perfect gift is from above, coming down from the Father of the heavenly lights.' Every gift of answered prayer is perfect, without fault, beautifully crafted and uniquely created just for us. It is precious, if we would only take the time to look inside.

The gift tells us about the giver

When my brother buys me DVDs with the cellophane removed, it tells me that he knows a good film when he sees one. He's clearly watched it before he wrapped it up! When a distant relative buys me a tin of biscuits at Christmas, I know that, as kind as it is, they don't really know what to buy me. When my wife buys me the *Infographic*

---

3 So glad God didn't answer my previous umpteen prayers for particular women to marry me, before I met 'The One'.

Bible, I say 'Wow!' because I didn't know it existed, and it's the perfect gift. And aren't those the best gifts? The ones that you don't even ask for, but the person buying it loves you so much and knows you so well that they get you your dream gift without even a hint of an Amazon wish list. I know for a fact God loves to give us these.

Back in 1999, I was looking to move to the Midlands to plant a church, but I needed work. I remember driving back from a successful interview for a dream job – it paid well and gave me complete flexibility to serve the church. As I drove, I sobbed my thanks to God for giving me this opportunity that was better than I could ever have imagined. I felt the Holy Spirit whisper, 'Why are you so surprised?' And yet, God is always 'able to do so much more than all we ask or imagine, according to his power that is at work within us' (Eph. 3.20). God can do more than we can imagine, but our response should still be to wonder at how intricately he knows us.

When I was young, I used to play a PC game called Football Manager. It's highly addictive to the point of being the most referenced PC game in divorce suits! I used to play this game so much that I finally broke the game disc and threw it in the bin. Twenty-five years later, and I find myself working on the coaching staff of a semi-pro team. One evening with friends, one of them tells me: 'My son was playing Football Manager the other day with your team.' 'Hang on,' says another, 'those games have all the backroom staff on.' He rushed to a PC, and a few searches later, I was looking at myself on Football Manager, full photograph, personal details, even a managerial rating. I cannot tell you how chuffed I was. The game that I had been utterly addicted to I was now a part of. Ecstatic doesn't come close – I think it's a bloke thing. For me, this was a blessing from God; in the midst of all that I was wrestling with at the time, he sent me the tiniest, most irrelevant encouragement, just because he knew how much it meant to me. In this moment, I was reminded once again that my Father in heaven understands me, even when I can't understand myself. He knows the intricacies of my mind and emotions, and he loves them. This one seemingly trivial gift reminded me of The Giver when I needed it most. And it was one thing to recognize the characteristics of God in that moment, but as I have taken the time to reflect on this occurrence, I discover more about him because the gifts of answered prayer are eternal, not temporary.

Gifts that get missed

There are many ways that we can often miss the full benefits of an answered prayer. First, there is the *overlooked gift*. How many times have we prayed for something and then forgotten what we have prayed for? This particularly happens with those unquantifiable answers touched on earlier in the chapter. Consequently, when the answer happens a few days, weeks or months later, we don't even recognize God's response to us. There is no 'wow' moment; it's like God is standing before us with a gift, and we take the benefit but just keep walking. No attention to The Giver and the opportunity to learn more about him unconsciously missed.

Second, there is the *short-term gift* – arguably the most 'wow-centric' approach. We hold the gift with wonder, we thank God for answering, for a few days maybe we are floating on the clouds elevated by the knowledge of his love. But then, after a while, the storms of life close in once more, and the gift is no longer remembered. It's like we throw it over our shoulder, discarded, erased from our memory. Perhaps subconsciously we view it as a short-term gift, great for the moment but, beyond that, having no lifespan – and in doing so we fail to explore the hidden riches that lie within that miracle. The eternity of truth held within is discarded. The value that it had for our future is lost, and once again The Giver is forgotten. My experience, though, is that the longer we can treasure the gift as time passes, the greater is our appreciation of it when we look back and remember.

Then there is the *gift refused*, when we don't like the answer and so instead of accepting it as God's wisdom, we harbour bitterness against God for what he is giving to us. It's perhaps particularly hard to look on this kind of answered prayer as a gift when it comes to praying for the life of a loved one and God says no. I received the most amazing answer to prayer from a couple who had lost their daughter at an early age, despite fervent prayer and petition. Ten years later, they were able to say with astounding peace that they were thankful for the no. In this deep valley of loss they suffered, they had found a greater intimacy with God together and discovered a depth of joy which was beyond the fluctuations of circumstance. A priceless gift. It is from this place of intimacy that they now trust that they will be united with their daughter for eternity.

There are also the *gifts rejected*. This so often happens when viewing the gift of others and is perhaps no better referenced than in the parable of the prodigal son when the other son says to his father, "Look! All these years I've been slaving for you and never disobeyed your orders. Yet you never gave me even a young goat so I could celebrate with my friends' (Luke 15.29). The older son rejects the gift and celebration for his younger brother under the dark shadow of jealousy, ignoring the father's expression of love to focus on the 'why not me?' question. As I've travelled around the churches, I've found this 'offended' response endemic, and we'll explore later on how it is powerfully preventing the sharing of God stories.

With each of these approaches to the gift of answered prayer, they miss out on the fact that when God gives, it has eternal value. When The Giver responds to our cries for help, his intervention is not short-lived; it has eternal ramifications if we seek to recognize it.

The eternal gift of answered prayer

Answered prayers shouldn't be like a Terry's Chocolate Orange. Allow me to explain. In our house on Christmas Day, the kids excitedly open their stockings finding the now inevitable chocolate orange.

The chocolate is usually consumed at about 5:30 a.m., and by the time their main presents are opened at 8 a.m., the orange is long forgotten. A euphoric experience enjoyed for a moment then forgotten. We can often be the same with answered prayer.

When the God of time and all creation chooses in his limitless understanding, unending love and sheer passion for us to answer a prayer, we have to be better stewards of that gift than my kids with the chocolate oranges – we shouldn't just move on to the next. Indeed, there are plenty of parables showing the value of using wisely what God gives us (Matt. 25.14–30) and encouraging us that if we do steward gifts wisely in God's economy, we should expect to see more. His master replied, 'Well done, good and faithful servant! You have been faithful with a few things; I will put you in charge of many things' (Matt. 25.23). Every answered prayer is a gift, packed with the DNA of God and sealed with his fingerprint, and so, as such, it cannot be temporary. The deeds of the God who operates outside the constructs of time cannot be limited merely to a moment. I believe each answered prayer is eternal in its power and meaning; its value never ends, never ages, never falls into irrelevance. It continues, if remembered, to tell of the intricacies of who God is, to reveal his nature and to declare to the listener what he is like. Testimonies don't need to be outstandingly miraculous to be a spiritual gift; if the story is of an answered prayer, it is by definition a Holy Spirit eternal moment, uniquely crafted for us to treasure.

Answered prayer: 2010

Emily and Sanju were expecting a child, and like most parents excitedly went to hospital for their 20-week scan, eager to have a first look at their baby. During the examination, the atmosphere changed as the nurse struggled to get a measurement for the baby's heart. Excitement transformed to despair as they were told there was a serious problem and they would need to come in for more tests. Deeply shocked, Emily and Sanju had experienced God answering their prayers multiple times so they turned to him once more. Their local church was superb, continuously praying for their baby to be healed. As the tests continued, it became evident that the problem could be life-threatening. Emily and Sanju were travelling into the hospital to get the results when Emily was crying out to God, begging him to heal her little girl. She felt him saying, 'Trust me, regardless of the circumstances,' and though deeply troubled, she felt peace. But the news from the hospital was not good; their baby had hyperplastic heart syndrome, incurable and ultimately fatal. They continued to pray. On 21 July 2010, Joy was born. The first few weeks were tough; she had an operation on her heart and then spent months in intensive care. Emily at this point was struggling in her faith: *What was the point in praying so much if Joy wasn't going to get well?*

Over the months that followed, Emily and Sanju were able to take Joy home. Bit by bit, day by day, despite all the medical challenges, some normality was emerging in their home, and life was beginning to be what they had dreamed for. But one day, mother's instinct led Emily to believe her baby was not all right. Then Joy started to cry and wouldn't be comforted, before she then stopped breathing. Emily had dreaded the day of losing her daughter, and now it had arrived. In shock, she and Sanju were devastated, yet despite this incredible depth of pain, they felt 'a strong sense of peace' as they felt God really close to them.

Eight years on, this incredible couple are grateful for their experience. Emily feels that God gave her the strength to overcome her greatest fear and that they have 'gained more through their grief than they have lost'. Their faith testifies that they prayed and God answered no, but in that, they have developed an incredible intimacy with Jesus and incredible peace that is as real to them as the pain – and a joy that cannot be snatched away from them through circumstances. God has, as promised to his people in Isaiah 61.3, bestowed 'on them a crown of beauty instead of ashes, the oil of joy instead of mourning'.

Practical steps

1 Take one of the answered prayers or moments when God touched your life, from your notes in Chapter 1, and begin to meditate on it.
2 Get a notebook and write down the story in full. Capture the context and all the detail you can.
3 Write down what you have learnt about God from this story and datestamp it. As you repeatedly come back to this story over the years, you will learn more about him, so add these revelations and date them too and see your understanding of God grow.

5
Perfect for you

History repeats itself, but the special call of an art which has passed away is never reproduced. It is as utterly gone out of the world as the song of a destroyed wild bird.
(Joseph Conrad)

Olive was on her way to the hairdresser when she realized she had left her hearing aids in. As they weren't allowed to get wet, she removed them and placed them in her handbag. Some hours later when she returned home, she looked in her handbag and only one hearing aid was there. During the next week, Olive searched everywhere, retracing her steps, and with no second hearing aid in sight, she went to order a replacement. She sat in the car so frustrated with herself and she prayed, 'I know I'm an 82-year-old woman, but Lord please help me.' Then she felt God speak to her, 'Go to Queenborough Petrol Station.' Olive was perplexed. 'What!?' Again she heard God's voice, 'Go to Queenborough Petrol Station.' And so nervously she went there and approached the cashier, 'It's a silly question, but have you found a hearing aid?' 'Yes,' she said. 'Someone handed it in. I put it on the shelf. It's been there all week.'

I was listening to a preach on the way to a business meeting, and they were sharing miracle stories of people finding things like the one above. To a sympathetic ear, these are great stories, but to those who have suffered loss and grief, they can create frustration and anger. Why answer this prayer and not the 'more important' ones? The simple conclusion could be that God listens to everyone else but not you. We know from the Bible that that isn't true. Instead, the question we may need to be asking was *why did God answer that person's prayer in that particular way?* I believe there is always something we can learn about the unique way God chooses to bless us all as individuals. Why did God answer that prayer, in that way, with that timing, with that outcome? If we can uncover at least some of these truths to remember, it could have a lifetime of impact rather than the glib 'Because he knows best.'

God is writing your story

The author of our life story
GOD made my life complete

when I placed all the pieces before him.
When I got my act together,
he gave me a fresh start.
Now I'm alert to GOD's ways;
I don't take God for granted.
Every day I review the ways he works;
I try not to miss a trick.
I feel put back together,
and I'm watching my step.
GOD rewrote the text of my life
when I opened the book of my heart to his eyes.

Psalm 18 (Paraphrase from *The Message*; MSG)

How exactly does God write the text of our life or, as Hebrews 12.2 puts it, perfect our faith? We know that he knew us even as we were 'knitted in the womb' (Ps 139.13), but do we believe that Jesus is writing the story of our faith? Do we believe that on the journey of life, he is seeking to perfect our faith? Just take a moment to consider this proposition, that the Lord Jesus Christ is focusing his attention, his love and his mercy on writing a story of faith in your life. It could be said that the narration begins the moment that we make the decision for Christ, although we also know that we were chosen before the creation of the earth. It's also clear that the decisions that we make using the free will that the Lord has given to us can heavily influence our faith story and there are certainly storms of life that occur along our path, sometimes of our own making, sometimes due to others. But we know that 'in all things God works for the good of those who love him, who have been called according to his purpose' (Rom. 8.28).

One of my friends often says, 'It's not all about you, you know,' to which my response is, 'I don't know; I think it probably is!'

At first hand, this seems like an incredibly arrogant statement to make, but what I'm trying to communicate is that I do have this deeply held belief that the world unfolds around us in ways that develop our walk with Jesus. It's a sense that God is able to write billions of people's faith stories all at the same time. Through his immeasurable intellect, unsurpassable knowledge and never-ending wisdom, he is able to weave all these stories together in such a way that his overall purpose for humanity is outworked. But he does this in such a way that will individually allow our faith and knowledge of him to develop. He works all things for the good of those who love him (Rom. 8.28) and he has no favourites (Rom. 2.11), so he is able to author millions of faith lives concurrently in such a way that each one has prominence and priority because of his deep love.

The threads of life

If God is creating a huge tapestry over history that points to Jesus, we are all individual threads in that masterpiece. Each unique singular thread has an impact on the whole picture, and so with his unending intellect, each one is crafted into the creation perfectly. Brilliantly and beyond our comprehension, these threads are not only connected but interact and influence each other, and yet the destiny of the overall theme remains unchanged. God has a unique and distinct plan and purpose for our lives, and if we are willing, the circumstances and environment that have an impact on us add the right colour and form to the thread as 'every detail of our lives is continually woven together to fit into God's perfect plan of bringing good into our lives' (Rom. 8.28, *The Passion Translation*; TPT). In other words, I was right, it *is* all about me; the world revolves around me so I may glorify him with the thread of my life. It just so happens, though, that it's also all about a few other billion people as well, all at the same time. God's wisdom is magnificent.

Meditate on that for a moment: the creator of the universe is the author of your faith story, and it's a story that you can co-write with him. As we reflect on our lives, we can view all the twists and turns, all the coincidences, chance happenings and the people that we have met that have brought us to this point in time and see how God has been working. Had I not known my Uncle Roger, I wouldn't have become a Leicester City supporter, which influenced me to go to Leicester University, where I met my girlfriend, whose dad helped me get a job at the very place where one of my colleagues invited me to church.[1]

Why, when, what, who?

Within the exclusive story thread of our lives, there are distinct exceptional moments when God moves and answers prayers in a way that signposts our direction of travel. Why does God answer prayer in the way he does and when he does? What dictates the timing and nature of the answer?

Consider for a moment a time when God answered a prayer for you. Why did he do it that way? Why did he do it when he did? If we believe that he is the author of our faith, then it follows that there is a divine purpose behind every story of answered prayer, and it is this that we should remember. When God intervenes, it cannot be anything but perfect. He is God and he does not make mistakes; his timing is not off. So why does God answer in the affirmative for people who pray for something that is lost, and others in the negative? His focus is on the journey of faith, the development of our walk with him, the honing of our character. The motivation in those flawless moments is the perfecting of our salvation, which is far above responding in a transactional nature to our calls.

The perfection of the story

I often come across people who are not willing to share their story because it hasn't yet 'perfectly been fulfilled'. But shouldn't we

---

1 Goodness knows what could have happened if I chose to support Derby County.

be celebrating every step of the journey with the God whose timing is perfect? When God stopped the disease in my spine, it was a miracle – he did what the doctors couldn't do. And yet, my spine is not perfect; it still shows the effect of having that disease for so many decades. I choose to declare the miracle believing that I will see it in its fullness. 'Being confident of this, that he who began a good work in you will carry it on to completion until the day of Christ Jesus' (Phil. 1.6). Let us credit God for all he has done, believing that each answer in his economy is perfectly enacted, perfectly timed in the perfect place for his purposes. If we were able to piece together every answered prayer through the history of time, we would have a greater understanding of who our master craftsman, creator and saviour is. Conversely, every story lost robs the world and time of that revelation. Every story has hidden within it a precious revelation of the infinite Lord of all.

The infinite attributes of God

I remember, having only been a Christian for a few weeks, listening to a teacher by the name of Roger Aubrey as he lectured on the attributes of God. I was 21, and it was the first time in my life that I realized that education could be interesting.[2] Sitting still and being quiet was not really my thing, but here I was hanging on every word as he explained who God was and what he was like; every morsel of information was so amazing. It seemed that every sentence challenged all I had ever thought of God – bombs exploding, blowing up my misplaced, misinformed views.

As explosion after explosion was going off in my head, Roger then moved to the question 'How big is God?' He proceeded to explain

---

2 Apologies to Chunky, Metal Mickey, Foggy and Brillo, who, despite their best efforts to try and teach me at secondary school, only managed to capture my attention long enough to be worthy of a nickname.

that everything that had ever happened, was happening and was ever going to happen, was all within the construct of time. Then he held before us a pin and said to imagine that all of time was in the pinhead – and that, relative to the pinhead, the room we were in could not contain God. Nor could the building, nor the city, nor the skies above – that's how big God is. I began to grasp, as much as you ever can, the infinite nature of God. God is infinite in his attributes. So what does that sort of infinite look like?

I imagine it like this: there is a book on the floor entitled 'God's love', and on top of it another book which describes a further aspect of his love, and above this another and another. And as each book reveals unique depths of his love, if you don't read every book, you will never attain a complete understanding of God's love. The problem is that the pile of books stretches on for infinity; it never ends as there is always more to learn about his love. And that's only the first aspect of God being infinite in his attributes; next to the pile of books on God's love is a stack of books on God's mercy, and in the same way, this pile reaches up into the heavens and onwards into infinity. Next to God's mercy is God's grace, next to God's grace, God's compassion. And the line of the piles of books about his attributes extends as far as the eye can see and beyond, off into the never-ending distance. God's attributes are not only infinite in their depth and capacity, but also in their number. Each of the attributes of God is infinitely limitless in its revelation of who he is, and the list of attributes itself is endless. If we studied a characteristic of God each day, and by some miracle were able to completely understand it, the time continuum would still not have enough days in it for us to fully discover each characteristic of our mysterious, unending, unfathomable God.

How can we represent the unfathomable?

I find it curious that some think they can not only fully understand the incomprehensible God, but also, as finite creatures, fully represent him in his infinity. Individually, we cannot do this, nor can one particular church, denomination or collection of churches, nor can even one faithful generation. It is beyond us. I'm grieved when I meet people who, when talking about a particular church, stream or denomination, concentrate on what they don't do rather than how they represent God well: *They don't do community. They are very insular, they don't evangelize. Their teaching has no practical outworking . . .* Is it realistic for any individual church in this fallen world to fully represent our omniscient, omnipotent God? Nope – just not possible. However, each church can represent him well in the particular facet(s) for which they have a burden and a God-given passion, and as the churches work together, so they present to the world a more accurate, if not complete, picture of who he is. And I believe it is the same for individuals. Instead of looking at each other with a spirit that casts judgement on their 'Christian performance', why not instead focus on how well we represent God? Listening to our brothers' and sisters' answered prayers, our eyes can be opened to different facets of God's nature. I encourage you not to harbour a hard heart against anyone in the church, but instead when you meet them, simply ask them to share one of those stories of answered prayer. Though representing the unfathomable, endless, omnipotent omnipresent is in its entirety out of our reach, being ambassadors for facets of his nature is entirely accessible.

Communicating the attributes of God through answered prayer

Most diamonds have 58 facets, which is 58 angles by which you can look at the jewel and have a flat side facing you. Imagine God as this incredible jewel with an infinite number of facets, limitless ways that we can see him and learn about him. Now let's link that to the concept of answered prayer. If each answered prayer is a unique gift imbibed with the DNA of God, then there is no excuse for devaluing our testimonies. I have sadly seen stories shared that have been met with misplaced complacency as it's one that's already been heard. But the same outcome does not necessarily have the same meaning; the same type of answer may reveal widely different aspects of God. For example, raising someone from the dead 'stories', though rare, are never even remotely similar. I have heard of a woman being raised from the dead as a young Christian teenager prayed and the whole village turned to Christ.[3] Then in contrast, I have heard of a man in Birmingham praying for his dad, who had died and was lying in a heap at the bottom of the stairs. As he cried out, 'Please let him die with dignity, God, not here like this.' The man came back to life, and the doctor was so shocked that he fell through the glass door. The family carried the father to his bed, said their goodbyes, and he died peacefully only a short time after. For me, the first account displays the power of God over death, leading to many salvations; the second reveals more of his deep compassion.

We know that God's answered prayers are not a mistake or haphazard, and so every single answered prayer, every single moment when heaven touches earth, is perfectly timed, flawlessly delivered and uniquely crafted. Though we don't always understand, we can be assured of the fact that this exceptional and exclusive moment is

---

3   Well, the whole village, that is, apart from the husband who was not that keen on his wife coming back to life.

there to reveal the Father's nature to us, not merely an answer but part of a narrative where the sovereign author unfolds another chapter on the journey of revealing who he is. It follows therefore that each testimony has no other like it; it is matchless in its disclosure of God's nature. If we choose to ignore it, we ignore him, forget it we forget him or hide it we hide him; that 'big reveal' is lost for ever this side of heaven.

Perhaps we would take more care with our answered prayers if we considered them each as a story which is entrusted to our keeping to be shared with those we meet. When I knelt by the side of my bed, at the age of 11, with no understanding of who God was, God responded, and then some. What does that tell us about who he is? I don't yet fully understand all that this response reveals of his nature, but I will keep telling the story and let the Holy Spirit do the revealing. If we could only grasp the preciousness and eternal value of the moment when God intervenes in our lives, it would be a game changer. If we could comprehend perhaps only a miniscule fraction of the saturation of purpose that lies in that moment, it could transform the way we view, behave towards and remember these God instances. There was a woman once who had a problem with bleeding; she had heard of this bloke Jesus who healed, and something rose up in her, some faith which said 'If I only touch his cloak, I will be healed' (Matt. 9.21). She managed to do so, and she was healed. She had no idea in that moment that her story would echo through the centuries and inspire millions of Jesus followers. I'm sure it never entered her head that this simple act of faith would be a catalyst for many to choose to believe in Christ. Though our individual experiences can in no way compare to the infallible word of God, the truth that they hold can ripple through time long after we are gone. As the psalmist exclaimed, 'Depths of purpose and layers of meaning saturate everything you do. Such amazing mysteries found within every miracle that nearly everyone seems to miss' (Ps 92.5, TPT).

Steward the answered prayer

Because each story of God at work in our lives is so precious, it needs to be stewarded wisely. So each story we have of God responding to our prayers shouldn't be cast away but preserved, not only for our own benefit but for the benefit of others. It's a piece of treasure to be shared, truth to be relayed – with the gift comes responsibility. When God answers our prayer, we have in our hands one of those facets of a diamond I referred to earlier, each reflecting a different insight into his nature. It is our choice what we do with that story. We can say, 'Thanks for the memory,' then throw it over our shoulder and walk away or maybe store the book to read from time to time for our own encouragement or others. As we choose to remember, understanding the beauty, uniqueness and eternal value of the moment is essential, and it should dictate what we remember. If we can take time to meditate on the moment to understand its inherent worth and clarify *what* we need to remember, then it will also help us to avoid praying for the same thing over and over again – that is, being stuck in the asking circle.

Answered prayer: 1954

Not long after June got engaged in 1954, she and her fiancé went to a high school football game. One can imagine her proudly showing off her ring to excited friends, but then at one point she looked down to see that the diamond from the ring had fallen out. Frantically, they looked all around them but could see nothing. They had been sitting on tiered bench seating with gaps that went to the grass below. June panicked and rushed out of the stadium to look under the tiered seating. Over the course of the night, hundreds of people had dropped their litter through the gaps – piles and piles of sweet wrappers, hot dog plates, old food. It was like trying to find a needle in a haystack. Overwhelmed, she prayed a simple prayer, 'Jesus, please help me find the diamond.' They went to the car to get a torch, and as they started to search, the torch caught a facet of the diamond. They got on their knees, searched through the grass and found it.

Practical steps

1 Take some time to reflect on the infinite attributes of God. Try to imagine that diamond, not with 58 facets but with infinite angles. Ask the Holy Spirit to expand your view of how big God is.

2 Ask God to highlight to you some moments in your past where he has intervened. Spend some time meditating on them – what makes them unique?

6
Stuck in the asking circle

Creance definition; a light cord attached to the leg of a hawk to prevent escape during training.[1]

---

1 Ok not the most inspirational of quotes but hopefully you'll see where I'm going. Read on.

Have you ever been in the situation where you are praying for the same thing over and over again? I don't mean in a persistent way, pressing into the holy of holies to find an answer, but rather finding yourself once again coming to him with the same problems years on from when you first started praying about it. These prayers may be dressed up in different situations, different circumstances, and different people, but essentially, they are just a repeat of an unchanged issue matched with an unchanged request to our father who answers. If we focus on what we remember from our answered prayers, I believe it can release us from a kind of Groundhog Day prayer life and into new spiritual depths in our journey with the Almighty.

An answered prayer for a fool

At the age of 21, I was fortunate enough to be able to buy my first house. Having had my bid accepted, I commissioned a full survey on the house, contracts were negotiated and the bank manager approved my mortgage. I was a few weeks away from my completion date when my tendency to not pay attention to detail reared its ugly head. Skim reading yet another legal document, I noticed it said No.13 Churchill Road. And then it dawned on me . . . I'd bought the *wrong* house. I'd never been in No.13; the house I'd looked round was No.32! Somehow, I'd got mixed up and was making my first step onto the property ladder with a house I'd never seen. No wonder the offer was accepted so quickly. Oh well, I was already committed . . .

A few weeks later, I walked into my new house for the first time with my good friends Pete and Crask. Being the super-zealous chaps that we were, we decided to pray in every room of the house: at the front door we prayed for a blessing for guests, in the lounge for good friendships to be forged, and in the study for wisdom. When we got to the kitchen, we opened the cupboards and prayed that they would never be bare and that we would always have enough provisions.[1]

At the time I was on a marketing graduate scheme and on good money, whereas both Pete and Crask were studying and skint. I shouldn't have been struggling for money, but a few months and a handful of dubious extravagances (including a *sunbed*) later, the cupboards were nearly empty. We remembered our prayers on the first day and with an air of indignation, we stood together to pray, asking our provider God, our Jehovah Jireh, to help us with food.

The very next day, Pete went to have coffee with a friend in the centre of Leicester. As they sat down, his friend explained that he had been praying that morning and felt that God has asked him to give Pete something. In the style of one of those shady spy films, he slid a small brown envelope across the table. As soon as the meeting ended, Pete ripped it open to reveal 25 crisp £10 notes. We had money for food, and that evening we praised God on full stomachs.

When I look back at that answer to prayer, I'm a little embarrassed. There is so much wrong with it: my lack of stewardship in buying the house, crazy spending on unnecessary items and then almost being cross with God because I didn't have enough food. What was I thinking? If ever three young men deserved *not* to have their prayers answered, that was the moment. And yet he did answer. I realize now how incredibly gracious God was to provide for us in such a special way. I wonder how many of us would have shown the same level of compassion, how many of us would have stepped in to help, or would we have stepped back so the hard lessons from the school of life – clearly lacking – could be learnt first?

It was the first time I can remember that God had provided for me in a practical way. It was exciting living in that moment, and inspiring to know that he was looking out for me. And yet, within a few months, my spending patterns reverted to type and after that, my

---

1 Goodness knows what we prayed for in the bathroom!

prayers were successive requests for divine bailouts. I had learned a simple truth at the time, that God could be active in my life, even in the most mundane elements of it. Only in recent times have I realized that there is also a greater truth in this answered prayer of provision which, had I grasped at that moment in time in 1991, could have transformed my life . . .

Remembering wrong

For decades after this miracle, I was stuck in a circle of asking God for provision, even quizzing him as to whether he was willing to do so. Fundamentally, I believe this was a consequence of misremembering how God had answered my first prayers for provision. The unique and eternal power embedded in an answered prayer is unlocked when we recall the right things. Our recollections can be detrimental when we 'remember wrong' , when our memory paints an incomplete picture of what occurred. We can 'remember wrong' *facts*. I was captivated by the film *Bohemian Rhapsody*, based on the life of singer Freddie Mercury, the lead singer of Queen, but I was probably the only person who watched it anticipating a particular twist at the end. I had some vague recollection that he had been shot so was expecting any moment for one of the characters to pull out a gun! It was a moving ending, but without an assassination. I got my facts wrong. A tactic of the enemy is to steal truth from us by way of incorrect recall. Right at the beginning of our history, in the Garden of Eden, we see the snake trying to encourage Eve to 'remember wrong'. 'Did God really say, "You must not eat from any tree in the garden"?' (Gen. 3.1) The 'devil is in the detail' may in some instances be true, but the 'divine is in the detail' too. Facts are important, and the recollection of them can dictate our direction.

Another way that our memories can be off is that although we remember the facts and the context of an answered prayer, we forget the *spiritual principle* that is embedded in the moment. Take a moment and think of the most outrageous story of God performing the miraculous in your life or the life of another – in the telling of the story, how much is focused on *why* God did it? The tendency we have to focus on the 'wow' and not the 'why' in our memories is an issue that Jesus deals with when with the disciples in Matthew 16.

It's not about the bread

When they went across the lake, the disciples forgot to take bread. (Matt. 16.5)

Can you imagine what it was like for the disciples in this moment? At some point on their journey, they have collectively realized that they have forgotten the bread, not once or twice, but three times. I can imagine them sailing across the lake, their minds consumed with worries: *What are we gonna do? How are we gonna eat? Who's gonna get the blame when Jesus finds out?* Perhaps they are grumbling with each other and finger pointing: 'It was *your* job to remember the bread! Soon Jesus is gonna realize, and then we're in for it. He's bailed us out a couple of times, but he's not gonna keep doing it – he'll hit the roof!'

'Be careful,' Jesus said to them. 'Be on your guard against the yeast of the Pharisees and Sadducees.' (Matt. 16.6)

Uh oh! #panic. There they were on the journey of their lives, travelling with a man who every time he opened his mouth, revelatory wisdom just poured out, words that gave them life and meaning. His words unravelled mysteries that had been hidden for centuries. There they were with the embodiment of love. There they were, and Jesus is about to reveal a new truth to them, fundamental to his very purpose. Jesus is about to reveal to them the prominence and prevalence of relationship over rules, love over religion, life-giving jewels from heaven – and what were they doing? There they were arguing and worrying about bread. It's not about the bread. Ladies and gentlemen, boys and girls, roll up, get your hearts ready – pin back your ears, it's time for a Jesus rebuke. And for the disciples (as ever) it's not what they expect.

> Aware of their discussion, Jesus asked, 'You of little faith, why are you talking among yourselves about having no bread? Do you still not understand? Don't you remember the five loaves for the five thousand, and how many basketfuls you gathered? Or the seven loaves for the four thousand, and how many basketfuls you gathered? How is it you don't understand that I was not talking to you about bread? But be on your guard against the yeast of the Pharisees and Sadducees.' (Matt. 6.8–11)

How on earth had the disciples forgotten the feeding of the five thousand and the feeding of the four thousand? The disciples had remembered wrong. I am incredibly forgetful. When we visit relatives, my wife even briefs me in the car on everybody's names: sisters, brothers, nephews, nieces. It often takes me 20 minutes to leave the house as I rush around trying to remember where I put my keys, wallet and phone – only to realize on minute 20 that my phone has been in my pocket all along.[2] But even I wouldn't forget that spectacular day when Jesus fed around ten thousand people with a handful of loaves and fishes.[3] Or would I? As I point the finger at those naive disciples, I see three fingers pointing back to me.

---

2 Irony not lost on me that God is birthing in me a passion for the tradition of remembrance.

3 Five thousand men were present in the scriptures; the number of children and women present is not recorded.

How on earth did they forget?

Perhaps they forgot the *facts*? *Did that miracle really happen? Did we really feed all those people? It doesn't make sense there were 12 baskets at the end. Maybe loads of the crowd did have food but didn't want to share it, and only got it out once some others were being fed. Maybe not so much of a miracle after all.* If we are not careful to capture every detail of any answered prayer we experience, the demons of doubt will deconstruct every element of it and remove what faith once stood in that place, leaving us with just a collection of happy coincidences.

Maybe they forgot the *context*? Perhaps they interpreted this miracle of Jesus as coming from different motivations, not out of compassion for the sheep without a shepherd (Mark 6.34), but thought it was a one-off bailout to get them out of trouble. Or maybe they viewed it as merely a demonstration of ability to reveal his purpose. For me, it is too far-fetched to believe that the disciples forgot the historical event itself, but what is undoubted is that they had either forgotten its spiritual significance, or not recognized it in the first place. They were stuck in a mindset of needing repetition rather than embracing the revolution that Jesus was bringing.

What really happened with the feeding of the five thousand?

Jesus had undoubtedly moved his revolutionary teaching of the disciples into a new phase, taking them from observers to partakers. When he sent out the 12 (Mark 3.13–19), it was a pivotal moment in his discipleship of them. For the first time in their adventure, they were to understand that the authority Jesus exercised was available to them as well. It was a *kairos* instant in the history of the world – a critical moment. Some Bible commentators see the feeding of the five thousand as being Jesus's miracle, sandwiched between the disciples experimenting in his authority (the sending of 12 and Peter walking on the water). But in truth, they are a divine trilogy of delegation, revealing his intention for his followers to extend the kingdom by walking in his footsteps. The miracle of the feeding of the five thousand came from the disciples' hands also.

The crowds were gathered to hear Jesus. When the problem of food arises, the disciples' instinct is to send the crowd to the villages, but it's a ridiculous suggestion. There's no way the surrounding areas could have coped with the demand. A human solution to this conundrum was not available; it was merely an attempt at dispersing the chaos and need to different locations. Often human solutions to spiritual problems just move the mess to somewhere else. But every impossibility, when embraced, is an opportunity to reveal the glory of the Father.

They look to Jesus; it's time for a heavenly bailout. They had already seen him turn water to wine, provide a bumper crop of fish, calm the storm. The danger is that Jesus becomes merely a solution giver. So form starts to develop, a structure that says when trouble hits, ask him to come to the rescue. Though the word is filled with encouragement to call on the Lord Most High in times of trouble, if we learn nothing from these times, then our view of God and relationship with him becomes nothing more than a 'shopping list deity' – wants and needs. We create a structure of religion, not one of deeper understanding with him. And this is where the disciples find themselves: 'Please, Jesus, get us out of this mess.' Significantly, Jesus pushes back: 'They do not need to go away. YOU give them something to eat' (Matt. 14.16). Time to do the maths.

If Jesus multiplied the bread in his hands and gave it to the disciples, who merely distributed it, that's a lot of work. It means they would give it to the 150 – 200 groups containing 50 to 100 people (Mark 6.40). We know that evening was coming, and by the time evening had arrived, they had all been fed and Jesus had retreated to pray (Matt. 14.23). So the time span is at best just a few hours. If the disciples were simply distributing the bread and fish Jesus was multiplying, they would each have had to go to Jesus over 500 times. They would have walked over 60 kilometres, pushing through the crowds back and forth – it would have taken them over 24 hours.[4] No. This miracle was a foreshadowing of the future: Jesus feeding the world through his followers. The disciples watched how Jesus did it and copied him. The Greek describes Jesus giving the bread to the disciples as a continuous action, and the same word is used as he encourages his 12 followers to do the same (Matt. 14.16). In other words, as they went to the groups, sat down and broke the bread, it multiplied in their hands too. The disciples performed a miracle. How on earth had they forgotten that?

A heavenly showoff?

Why does God perform miracles or answer prayers? There are clear lessons here in the feeding of the five thousand. We see that Jesus is not restricted to the laws of physics; rather, he is the Lord of physics. God can do anything; these miracles can still happen today in our age – and they do. Indeed, my friend whose husband invited more people round than they had food for experienced similar multiplication when she prayed over her soup for four and it stretched to fill 12 bowls, with more than enough left over. And another friend went to India and met a man whose cooker had only enough paraffin for two days and no money to refill it. He prayed over it – it lasted for four months. A colleague of mine at a Bible college in the States had a young student who experienced it when, unable to pay his fees, he prayed and woke up to find several diamonds in his bed (one alone worth $20,000)! And yet, when reading of such miraculous occurrences, we can fall for the same trap as the disciples. It's all about the bread; the focus is on the 'wow' and not about the 'why'. We too often wonder at God's actions and miss his *motivation*. We know Jesus fed

---

4 This all assumes perfect order and excellent administration. Something I have yet to experience at religious gatherings of over 20 let alone ten thousand people.

the five thousand out of compassion, but his *modus operandi* was a revelation that the disciples could exercise mind-blowing levels of authority through him. When God answers prayer and intervenes in our lives with a miracle, he does so for a reason and not to show off. Every divine intervention does not merely demonstrate his ability, but declares his intention towards us.

If we focus on the Hollywood moment, we miss the meaning of the film

God is more interested in our journey of faith than the occasional motorway services pit stop of an answered prayer. Let our remembrance be focused not on the 'what' but more importantly the 'why'. It's not the moment of 'wow' when God conspicuously interacts in our life, but it's the journey before and after the 'wow'; it's what we learn about the nature of Jesus during our travel which should dominate our attention. Fixing our sights exclusively on the 'wow' of answered prayer without giving any focus to the 'why' is like watching a highlight package of a football game but never knowing the score. It's like revering the escape moment in *Shawshank Redemption*[5] but never watching the rest of the film, capturing the Hollywood moment but missing the meaning. These God moments, these instances of intervention, will be an opportunity missed if the totality of our remembering consists of the physical response for all to wonder at. When we investigate the 'why', we discover the multiple layers revealing the wisdom of The Giver. We're called to remember beyond the action to discover the intention.

5 Spoiler alert – oops, sorry.

God's intention through answered prayer

Have you ever prayed for God's provision? Has he answered? If so, he has declared his intention of being your Jehovah Jireh, your provider. He is the God who never changes, unlike mankind. 'God is not human, that he should lie, not a human being, that he should change his mind' (Num. 23.19) and 'the same yesterday and today and forever' (Heb. 13.8). So, as you come before him for daily bread, there is no foundation to doubt his personal purposes for you, nor his intentions toward you. A spiritual amnesiac prays with panic for bread, not knowing if God will answer; the one who remembers prays filled with faith and anticipation. As we move onto maturity in our prayers, we should do so in confidence of his intentions.

I look back with regret on the amount of my prayer life that has been dominated by my own need and my own lack of faith as to whether God wanted to meet it. Doubt cannot coexist in a prayer with the knowledge of certainty of his nature. There are mysteries of God to discover, and all I have done is invest my time focusing on having the finance to buy a pizza. Bill Johnson says, 'when we have experienced the provision of God, it is illegal to begin a conversation with need.' When God provided for me and my friends back in 1991, we celebrated the 'wow', but it took me over 25 years to understand the 'why': Jesus's provision for me is motivated out of love. It is not based on my performance, cannot be influenced by my foolishness, but is rooted in his steadfast, unchanging, unhindered, unfailing love for me. I daily decide to move out of the asking circle, to seek first the kingdom and focus on the beautiful Jesus Christ – not my need.

Following his rebuke in Matthew 16, the penny finally drops; the disciples remember at last and not just the facts of what happened when and to whom, but a 'spiritual remembrance'. Among the chaos, the drama and the 'wow' of the moment, they captured in their heart the 'why'.

Then they understood that he was not telling them to guard against the yeast used in bread, but against the teaching of the Pharisees and Sadducees. (v. 12)

It was never about the bread. Over the following days with Jesus, the disciples peppered him with questions, faced numerous challenges and yet we see no evidence that they ever asked about or worried about provision again.

Conflicting scriptures?

So how does this view tally with the fact that Jesus instructs us to *ask* for our daily bread (Matt. 6.11) and commends the persistent widow for her repeated prayer (Luke 18.7)? At first look, it seems to conflict with Jesus's rebuke to the disciples. These seemingly opposing views can cohabit in the context of our journey with him as we work out our salvation (Phil. 2.12). It is good to continually ask God for our provision, but there should be a development in how we ask, a greater understanding of the nature of the giver. As the writer of Hebrews puts it, we should be 'taken forward in maturity' (6.1). Our conversations should progress from asking for physical provision with hints of 'if it be your will', to a growing confidence and a prayer in faith in the assurance of knowing God's intentions. The effectiveness of a prayer girded by the understanding of past requests and answers is greatly increased over one full of doubt, tossed about by life's latest storm (Jas. 1.6).

There are times on our journey where God calls us to persist in prayer to discover more, but if we do so on matters that are already established, where his intention is already declared, then we are stuck. To this end, I find it fascinating that those who are called to intercede do so at a different level; their focus and attention is to pray for deeper knowledge, wisdom and understanding. The prayer battles for legends like Rees Howells were not for petty provisions but for the destiny of nations, and the salvation of millions. We are called higher when we remember the 'why'.

Releasing the creance

To understand how we can go higher, let's look at falconry, the ancient art of training a bird of prey to hunt with its master. During the training, the hawk responds only to food. Once the hawk is a few weeks old, it is taken out on a leash known as a creance. Initially on a short leash of no longer than a metre, the hawk jumps on the ground to follow a leather lure which has meat attached to it and soon learns that food comes from the master. Over the following weeks, the leash is extended and the hawk is able to fly circling the master and capturing its food on leather lures swung in circles high above the master's head. At its maximum, the hawk can fly to a height of 15 metres on a creance in this type of training. After a relatively short time of three months in its training, the hawk is let off its leash, the creance is released and the hawk is free to fly, but it always returns to the master. The red-tailed hawk has been known to fly 2,500 metres high.

The lessons we learn from answered prayer should not only centre us on God but also free us from earthly concerns in the knowledge that he has it in hand. We then have a choice. We can depend on heavenly bailouts, circling the master like a weeks-old hawk waiting expectantly, staying at that level of faith and focusing our relationship with him around need. Or we can remember our answered prayer in detail, the facts, the context and, critically, the spiritual meaning – take to heart the 'why' Jesus has intervened in our lives – and use that building block of faith and fly higher, confident in God's provision. The creance is released, and we have an adventure before us; let's not circle at low level, when we have been off the leash all this time. Each story we remember not only has within it a power to release us to great heights, it carries an eternal divine principle that acts as a catalyst for the miracle to happen again.

Answered prayer: April 2019

In her final year of university, Emelyne fell seriously ill with a flu-like virus. Within a week, she went from being well and enjoying her studies to not being able to walk. In the months and years that followed, she never fully recovered. She lived daily with a range of symptoms including fatigue, muscle and joint pains all over her body, migraines, nausea and sensitivities to light and sound. She was diagnosed with myalgic encephalomyelitis/chronic fatigue syndrome – a chronic health condition with no cure and no recognized treatment. It was not at all how she'd expected her adult life to start.

Over seven years, through the daily pain and struggles, she always had a sense that God was holding her up. One week when she was particularly bad, her mum encouraged her by committing that they should pray together for her to be well. It was a challenge because over the years, she had found her private prayers very much focused on others, not herself. In truth, this was really the first time she had prayed to be well. She felt Jesus speak to her: 'Ask and you shall receive, seek and you shall find, knock and the door will be opened to you.' That weekend with her mum she visited Ffald-y-Brenin, West Wales, a peaceful retreat centre in the countryside. After the midday prayer meeting, she lay down on the floor of the prayer room, hoping for a power nap. But pain was surging throughout her body. She felt it pushing towards her head and to her feet, so much so that she kicked off her trainers. It continued to surge. Then, in a moment, she heard God speak, 'I'm evacuating, evacuating, evacuating the illness from you.' At the same time, she saw above her a pair of infra-red scanners attached to hands, scanning the length of her body, seemingly extracting the illness from her. She knew in this moment God had answered her prayer, and over the next three weeks, her body was freed of the sickness. On the morning of the miracle, Emelyne had read and prayed Psalm 30, 'LORD my God, I called to you for help and you healed me.' It was a prayer that changed her life, as God answered.

Practical steps

1 Consider an issue that you seem to be repeatedly praying for.
2 Is there a time where God has answered a prayer of this nature in the past? If so, review it – what does this tell you about his intentions towards you?
3 Search the Scriptures to see his will on the matter.
4 Believing that God's intentions to you do not change, bring this issue to him again, but this time thank him for what he has done for you personally, declare his intentions through his Scripture and let faith and assurance of his purposes for you and others build.

7

Are you an again believer?

Jesus Christ is the same
yesterday and today
and forever.
(Heb. 13.8)

Are you an again believer? I don't mean a born-again believer; I mean do you believe that if God has done it once, he can do it again and again and again? I think it's easy to believe in Jesus, but much harder to believe *him* – that is, to believe him at his word. It doesn't take much faith to say I believe in Jesus Christ; it's much harder to put your trust in him in real life. It's one thing to know that Jesus can heal; it's another to take the risk and pray for your friend's broken leg today. When we believe Jesus as opposed to believing in him, we expose ourselves to the risk of the supernatural. As author Shawn Boltz says, we should 'trust God enough for [our] resources to not live a normal version of [our] calling'. Imagine you're going to see a cliff. You have two options:

Option 1: stand at a safe distance away from the 100-ft drop with something to hold on to.

Option 2: stand at the edge of the cliff, so your toes have only air around them and you feel like you might fall – and then jump.

Option 1: believe in Jesus – safe, secure. Option 2: believe him at his word – jump. Trust in him and only him. It's terrifying. But it is in these moments that we find true intimacy with the creator of the universe.

There have been multiple times when my wife and I have jumped. You know the moments where in your heart you know God has asked you to do something – a feeling, a prompting – and though you are surrounded by a thousand facts that tell you it's madness, you take a deep breath and go for it. It's high risk; you know you could crash and burn at any instant, but you don't want to die wondering, so you choose to trust in the only one who can help. This is believing Jesus. I'm not one who goes for the concept of blind faith, jumping and just hoping. No, we jump in the knowledge that though we can't see the answer, or understand the 'how', the God of the again is with us. I would be powerless to take that risk without being an again believer.

Placing myself in a situation of being utterly dependent on him is founded on educated and informed faith, fuelled by my experience and others' accounts of God's works. The Scriptures not only show God repeating miraculous deeds, but indicate that the sharing of stories of answered prayers can actually be the catalyst for God's miraculous interventions.

The multiplier effect

When visiting Bethel Church in Redding, California, I bumped into a guy called Dave Harvey who shared my passion for sharing testimony. Dave told me a story of how, while in a meeting with some Christian friends, he was struck by the sense that God wanted to give each of them $1,000. He shared this with the group – and no doubt a few eyebrows were raised – but by the end of their time together, there was already an envelope placed on the table with one of the group members' names on it and $1,000 inside. Over the next few days, each member of the group received money in different ways: a promotion and $1,000 raise; cash taken to the bank to pay in the day's takings increasing by $1,000 by the time it reached the till, and so on. It was a crazy list of occurrences, but within a few days, each one in the group had received $1,000 in one form or another.

The concept that Dave introduced me to was that God could 'do it again', and he shared with me multiple stories of how he had seen miracles replicated following the telling of the stories. When I shared the story with my family back home, my wife, of fuller faith than I, said somewhat indignantly, 'What about us? I'm going to pray for £1,000 each.' Nothing happened.

A few months later, and once again money was tight. I had pencilled some time off for holiday but had no idea where we would go and certainly no finance to book the luxury of a break abroad. We had £1,000 put aside, but this was during a school holiday so at best we were looking at a weekend in Skegness. Nothing wrong with that, but I was *exhausted*. I'd ploughed so much of my physical, emotional and spiritual energy into work that I was on empty. I was desperate to lie in the sun and do nothing – the weather forecast for Skegness was not good. Then, Sarah told me that she felt we needed to give the £1,000 to someone for their holiday, but she didn't know who and felt it would be at the European Leaders Alliance conference we were now headed for. We took the money out of the bank, put it in an envelope and set off for the conference.

As I filled the car up for the journey, I felt a little nudge from the Holy Spirit: 'Every time you go to this conference, you get challenged.' Stewing on the words and wondering what battle was ahead, I went to the till and presented my debit card for payment. It was rejected. So I gave my credit card. It was rejected. We had no money. The temptation to dip into the £1,000 was massive, but Sarah and I agreed it was a no-go; it wasn't our money anymore. Somehow, we managed to cobble enough cash together to pay for the petrol, but it meant we were about to go to a three-day conference without a bean to our name. I was embarrassed – here I am, standing in front of two thousand people, about to share the vision for a multimillion-pound monument to encourage the nation to pray, and I couldn't even afford a cappuccino for my wife. But the conference was great, and each day people offered to buy us coffee or sandwiches, with no idea what it meant to us. Then I saw a couple and felt a Holy Spirit nudge that these were the ones that Jesus wanted us to bless with holiday money. I have to say they didn't really fit into my giving paradigm; they were a beautiful young couple, very well-dressed, and they certainly didn't look short of cash. I wanted us to give the money to a poor couple who had never had a holiday, whose minds would be blown away by God's generosity. I told Sarah – she was not impressed. But we prayed and both felt they were the right couple to give the money to.

I approached them and gave them the envelope, telling them it was for their holiday, and walked away. After opening it and seeing the gift, they rushed after me and proceeded to tell me that only ten minutes previously someone had prophesied that they would receive a gift for their holiday today. Wow! What a confirmation that we'd found the right couple. But then the couple told me how they had overstretched their holiday budget, and this would now help them with their spending money as they went to Mauritius. *Mauritius? Mauritius!* I smiled, but inside I was wrestling with God. But he affirmed we were doing the right thing. It made little sense to me, but I decided to trust instead of arguing.

That evening, the preacher talked about finance, and tearfully, Sarah and I went forward for prayer, holding each other's hands. The preacher came and prayed for us, laid his hands on us and said that God was going to give us a surprise. On our way back home, the debit and credit cards started working again, and I contemplated a few days admin and finding a way to get a holiday. I soon read some notes from a Rick Warren preach who said that when you're praying, you have to act like you have already received it. 'Ok, then,' I thought, 'time to act.' It was now seven days before our scheduled break, and I was going to the travel agents!

Walking into the travel shop, I told one of the staff members I wanted to grab a last-minute deal to go on holiday the next Friday. She excitedly dived straight in and started asking about our holiday requirements. I was feeling even more nervous: 'Er, before we get started, there is just one small detail I probably ought to let you know . . . I don't have any money.' She peered over her glasses with a withering look before exchanging glances with a colleague that communicated one clear message: 'Time-waster.' She politely went through the motions, then asked me for my budget. I decided to go big – why not believe for the holiday of a lifetime? 'I'm looking for something between four and five thousand pounds,' I heard myself saying. More glances exchanged, subtle shaking of disapproving heads. 'When do I need to bring in the money?' Abruptly she replied, 'Two days.'

The following morning Sarah woke me up: 'You're going to want to see this!' Half asleep, I followed her downstairs where she pointed to the front door. There, typed on a piece of A4 paper, was a message: 'This is seed to eat, not seed to sow.' Surrounding the instruction were £20 notes – lots of them. We woke the children, and they came down to share in the amazement. We grabbed cash in handfuls, and the kids counted it into piles as they sat by the Monopoly board from the game they had played the previous day. And then we counted the bundles – it was £5,000! 'We're going on holiday, kids.' What thrilled me most was not so much the holiday, but the fact that my children at such an early age were able to see the God who can do it again. They were able to experience first-hand the thrill of believing Jesus because there are no other options. We had heard an incredible story of provision and owned it for ourselves; we had believed for an extravagance, and God had answered. How and why did this spark of faith received from hearing Dave's story lead us to this point of answer? What the heck had just happened?

The Scriptural logic puzzle

When it comes to the things of God, I like to keep it simple. I looked at the facts:

1 We know that God listens and answers prayer, both from Scripture (Jer. 29.12–13, Ps 66.17–20, 1 Pet. 3.12, 1 John 5.14) and from experience.
2 God never changes. It is impossible for him to do so – if he does, he stops being God.
3 God has no favourites (Rom. 2.11). This means that Mother Theresa, Billy Graham and the apostle Paul are all on the same level as little old me and you.

Next, I took Dave Harvey's answered prayer and lined it up with these three truths:

1 If I pray for $1,000, will God answer? Maybe not in the way I expect, but yes, answer he will.
2 Has God changed since he answered Dave's prayer? I can't really see how he could, no.
3 Is Dave better than me? Probably. But is he any more of a favourite to God than me? No.

This may seem childlike, but the Bible does encourage us to approach Jesus like a child, and I know by this logic, like I know in my heart, God can do it again. We see repeats of miracles multiple times in Scripture. In the parting of the sea (Exod. 14.21–22) and then the Jordan (Josh. 3.15–16), we see a similar miracle, but different expressions of faith from Moses and Joshua, respectively. The Lord instructs Moses exactly what to do: 'Raise your staff and stretch out your hand over the sea to divide the water so that the Israelites can go through the sea on dry ground' (v. 16). Undoubtedly, the faith needed was built on his previous experiences, but 'jumping' with God he was about to do a new thing. But in Joshua, the journey is different. God reassures Joshua that he has not changed, 'so that they may know that I am with you as I was with Moses' (v. 7), but the instruction is limited. They are only told to stand in the river, and yet because of the history of the parting of the sea, Joshua realizes that God is about to do it again. He has a different faith and boldness than Moses, in some respects. Compare God asking Moses 'Why are you crying out to me?' with Joshua's bold statement of what God was about to do, 'waters flowing downstream will be cut off' (Josh. 3.13). Joshua's knowledge of God's miracle through Moses emboldens him to believe for the same to happen again. We see a similar repetition in the lives of Elijah and Elisha, respectively (1 Kgs 17.14–16 vs 2 Kgs 4.4–5). It is, I contend, not by accident that we see the miraculous repeat in the ministry of Elisha; he has followed Elijah's ministry and called for a double portion. As he asks God to do it again, his faith is for greater and more, as he has already seen God do it once.

A caveat

God is the God of the again, but I'm not saying that he always will – that would be formulaic – but I am saying he always *can*. Clearly, there are countless times when God answers differently than we hope, times when he answers no, but often we disqualify ourselves from even asking God to repeat miracles: *He was different in Bible times; he can't do that now. He will do that for her, but not for me.* Part of the power of the testimony shared about is the recognition that we do not pray in a vacuum, we do not approach God from ground zero. Instead, reading or listening to the answered prayer of others stirs our faith; it's faith fuel. A story of something that Jesus has done shouts out a clear message: God has done it once, and he can do it again. This is not being stuck in the asking circle where our petitions have a flat-lined faith; rather, the more we hear stories of what God has done, our prayers are filled with increasing confidence. And if you're not convinced by this approach, would it persuade you if I told you that God demonstrates the same?

The 'As I's' of God

Often in the Old Testament, when God is trying to stir faith or warn the main protagonist of the story, he does so by telling them what he has previously done. God's methodology when reinforcing the point is to give examples of what he's done in the past, or to reveal himself as the same God now as the God of one of their famous ancestors. By inference, he is saying, 'All that I did then I can do again,' or, if you like, 'If you acknowledge I did that in the past, why not believe I can do the same in your present?' In Joshua 1.5 we read: 'As I was with Moses, so I will be with you; I will never leave you nor forsake you.' In 1 Kings 9.5: 'I will establish your royal throne over Israel forever, as I promised David your father when I said, "You shall never fail to have a successor on the throne of Israel."' And in 2 Kings 23.27 we read: 'So the LORD said, "I will remove Judah also from my presence as I removed Israel."'

In each of these situations, God is not delivering new information to the hearer. That's not the purpose of his communication – he is recalibrating the listener to who he is; he is reminding them of what he has done and reinforcing that if he has done it once, he can do it again. What he has done is a foundation for what he is going to do. We see this approach in 1 Chronicles 17.8: 'I have been with you wherever you have gone, and I have cut off all your enemies from before you. Now I will make your name like the names of the greatest men on earth.' The 'As I's' in the word of God are a powerful reference point for who he is. We can take this approach and incorporate it into our prayer life, but care is needed in doing so.

I believe God is the do-it-again God, but there is danger in approaching our prayer and petition to him with an arrogance of what he *should* do. For example, 'God, you did this miracle for him, so do it again for me.' Such an approach lacks humility and misunderstands the value of remembering as we draw near to him. The purpose of our remembrance is to build a thankful heart (Ps. 100.4) and to retune our spirit to his, realigning our senses with his. It means that as we call on him to do it again, we do so from a place of peace, armed with truth we have learnt from faith stories. Retelling is not just about increasing faith; it's about creating a spiritual atmosphere.

Remembering and prophesying

Bill Johnson teaches that every story has within it the spiritual power to replicate itself. 'For the testimony of Jesus is the spirit of prophecy' (Rev. 19.10, ESV). Now the word 'testimony' has been somewhat 'Christianized' – we hear it and think 'story of salvation', but that is not what the equivalent Greek and Hebrew words mean. Simply put, a testimony is an account, a telling of what has taken place. Johnson[1] explains that the written or spoken story of what Jesus has done, when read or heard, actually prophesies that God can do it again – it's not a vague hope, but a spiritual act. In effect, when we share a story of what God has done, we are declaring into the heavenlies for it to repeat; we change the spiritual atmosphere enabling that miracle to happen again. This means our God stories have the power to breathe life into any storm, just in the recollection of an answered prayer we can transform the environment and align it with heaven's destiny for those who listen. There is a spiritual power in every story. And it is with these power-packed spiritual dynamite stories that we can overcome. 'They triumphed over him, by the blood of the Lamb, and by the word of their testimony' (Rev. 12.11).

I heard an account from a vicar at St Andrew's church where he saw this principle in action. As one person shared a story of God's healing, someone in the congregation got healed just in the listening and praying in this changed atmosphere. Then that person shared what had happened, and again in the listening and praying in a changed atmosphere, someone else was healed. And so it went on all evening until in total 63 people gave testimony that night to physical healings. As each person gave testimony, more healing came to those waiting to give their testimony, and to people in the congregation. What we hold in our memories are not just stories to encourage our friends and families, but an explosive concoction of truth and intention that can radically alter any landscape for God's glory. Such things should not be held lightly.

I'm intrigued by the passage in Matthew 8.4, where Jesus heals the leper but warns him against sharing the story. 'See that you don't tell anyone. But go, show yourself to the priest and offer the gift Moses commanded, as a testimony to them.' Jesus understands the power that is released when giving an account of his works and does not want the consequential repetition and acceleration to take place before its time.

When I travel around churches sharing the vision of the Eternal Wall of Answered Prayer and telling stories of what God has done,

I have seen the power of sharing testimonies in action. I regularly share my own story of being healed of ankylosing spondylitis, and I see many healed of the same disease. One pastor insisted to his staff to go to a meeting I was at, prompted by the Holy Spirit; they told him he needed to rest. He had a crushed vertebra in his back and was in immense pain, but he felt compelled to go. When I shared my story with him, we humbly asked for God to 'do it again'. The pain disappeared and he was healed! And I have seen this happen over and over again. It doesn't work like clockwork – it's not a formula for spiritual success (any such approach is religion) – but it compels me to place a heavy value on telling people what Jesus has done. I had a meeting with a politician one day, and he shared with me how he and his wife had been struggling to conceive for many years. I sent him six stories of people who had been in similar situations, and together they read the stories and prayed in a different way to the God who answers. Nine months later, they sent me their God story following the birth of their beautiful daughter.

When God answered our prayer for holiday money, I had a decision to make. Do I tell anyone? Part of me said no. Spending that amount of money on a holiday was a complete extravagance. Maybe we should have donated it to charity? I was concerned it was going to offend many, but at the time we felt sure that is what God wanted us to spend the money on, and we praised him in private. If answered prayer is a gift that carries power, I cannot just hide it away. I shouldn't be ashamed of what God has done in my life nor conceal how he has blessed me. And if I believe in the God of the again, the multiplication of the miracle, then surely I have to share it so that others can experience it too? With deep breaths, I posted it on Facebook.

Before long, one of my closest friends called me and rebuked me; she knew we were struggling and felt it was madness to spend the money on a holiday. Social media then weighed in: *Nonsense! Fake money! Give it to charity!* My football friends were concerned it was drug money, that somebody had put it through the wrong letter box. There were a few 'wow' and 'praise God' comments, but people were not impressed. The following Sunday, I shared the testimony at church and asked those in need to stand. I prayed that the God of provision, the God of the again, could do it for them too. Immediately afterwards, a woman shared how she had seen the post on Facebook and showed her children. They wanted to move house and needed a big chunk of money. Her son said, 'Mummy, why can't God do that for us?' She replied that he could, and they all prayed together as a family. Later that afternoon, they received a call to let them know that a long-lost relative had passed away and left them a large inheritance. Over the weeks and months, many came back to me and shared stories of how the miracle had multiplied. I am not here proposing a prosperity gospel, nor some quick fix to getting prayers answered. I'm merely trying to communicate a simple truth: each story of answered prayer has within it the power to multiply. If God can do it once, he can do it again. So, are you an again believer? Do you believe that the God of Moses is the God of today, that there is nothing which is beyond him, nothing that is too difficult for him? Do you believe that if God has done it once, he can do it again and again and again? Because if you do, that knowledge comes with a responsibility. Every Christian on this planet has a story of answered prayer – at the very least, they have the story of salvation and Jesus answering their cry for help, their plea for his lordship. We all have a story to tell, stories brimming with revelation of who God is, and so we need to take extreme care not only in what we remember but also in how we do it, stewarding these Godly memories wisely.

Answered prayer: 2014

Zac and Sarah were expecting twins, but at the 20-week scan were told that twin number two was missing part of his brain at the back called the inferior cerebellar vermis. Over the next few weeks, Sarah was having two scans a day, and it was clear that the doctors were doing all they could to ensure both twins would survive. They were told by the consultant that the brain could not and would not grow back – it was impossible. Scan after scan confirmed the missing brain section. Sarah had a call from a friend who had been in a similar position, and they prayed. They prayed with friends, and Zac had a peace, 'You know God can do this.' He didn't know if he would but knew he could. The twins were born prematurely, the room filled with nurses and doctors because of the complications. Both twins had scans, which was standard procedure. Later that day, a junior doctor in passing just said to Zac and Sarah, 'Scans have come back, everything's fine.' *What?* Another junior doctor ran down the corridor shouting, 'The brain, it's all there!' The brain had miraculously, impossibly regenerated itself. Now, many years later, twin number two – Finley – leads a full life. Thank you, God.

Practical steps

1 Meditate on Revelation 12.11 and Revelation 19.10.
2 Take one story of answered prayer in your life and meditate on it and the fact that it can happen again.
3 Pray for a friend that this story will be replicated in their lives.

Part 3

HOW CAN WE REMEMBER?

8

Choosing to consolidate our God memories

We are too prone to
engrave our trials
in marble and
our blessings in sand.
(Charles Spurgeon)

Why is it that we can remember some things and yet not remember others? Why can I remember, for example, that Leicester City lost 3-1 in the FA Cup against Millwall in 1986? Why can I remember my best friend Wayne Harris's phone number from school? And yet other things are a complete blur. I struggle to remember my wife's birthday, and when the bank uses it as my security question, I ask them if I can phone a friend. Why can I never remember the name of a person I've met less than two seconds after they have told me? How do our brains choose what we remember and what we forget?

Now, at this point I am going to politely ask any brain surgeons to skip this chapter as I attempt to dumb down neuroscience for the purposes of the rest of us.[1] Every single moment of our lives, our brains capture and store the details of that moment. Let's say it's like we have a mass of empty shelves in our brains, and every single fact, experience and sensation creates a book on the shelf. Now, if those shelves stayed full, we wouldn't be able to cope with the overload of information that we have access to. Imagine just a day of capturing and retaining every memory. Every word we heard spoken, every sight we had seen, every taste, every smell, every sound – it would be too much. For this reason, our brains have receptors to tackle this risk of excessive burden, and they are named DAMB and dDa1. That's way too scientific, so let's call them the brain librarians: Billie and Larry. Billie's job is to go along the shelves, take off the books and shred them; effectively, she helps us to forget. Larry's job is to keep the books there – he chains them to the shelves so Billie can't shred them and so that the moment is not lost; effectively, he helps us to remember. It's a continuing process, and Billie is quite an active gal, so she may return to some of the old books and if the chains have got rusty and weak, she will pull them out too. In parallel, Larry will also revisit some of the books and check the chains

---

1 Hello, brain surgeons – probably best for you to read this research and begin your rabbit hole here: <https://www.sciencedaily.com/releases/2012/05/120509180113.htm>.

are not weakening. How does Billie know which books to shred and which ones to leave? How does Larry know which ones to keep and continually strengthen? Also, why on earth didn't Larry put chains on the book entitled 'My Wife's Birthday'?

Jacob Berry, who discovered these receptors, said that the important memories are protected by the 'act of consolidation'. That is, they are shielded and retained when we mark them out as important. The value that we place on them and the regard we give them dictates whether or not they are stored, and remain stored, in the libraries of our mind. So the significance we place on a memory is effectively the chain that Larry uses to keep the book on the shelf. The more we revisit this memory, the stronger the chains.

Building memory libraries

The recent research review of Tyng[1] demonstrated that emotion can have varying impacts on our ability to remember. In some extreme emotions, our memory is shielded from us so we do not have to relive painful times; on other occasions, emotion is the consolidating factor. My earliest childhood memory is from a family holiday when I was aged around four. My mum had sent me to fetch my sister from the pool, as it was time for tea. I stood on the edge and leant over to shout for her, but I lost my balance and fell in. I didn't try to swim. I clearly remember serenely and slowly drifting to the bottom; I remember the blue and the silence. That moment is etched on my memory. I can go back there in an instant, and the whole experience gives me an eerie sensation. As an aside, you will be pleased to know I survived. A man in a white suit was walking by and jumped in to save me. Once he had rescued me out of the water, he disappeared as soon as he had arrived – make of that what you will. With extreme emotion excepted, whether it be fear, love, hate or joy, emotions communicate to our brains that the memory has significance, and it becomes consolidated. Even these consolidated memories need to be revisited to ensure they are reinforced over time. But the memories that we store are not merely at the behest of our emotions. From Berry's research, we can draw the conclusion that we can have an intentional impact on what we retain – it scientifically demonstrates that we can each have a significant influence on what we remember. If 'our memories are the real estate of the mind,'[11] we have the opportunity to build wisely, to create a landscape flooded with 'libraries' that glorify God. Remembering is not a haphazard occurrence beyond our control; it is a choice. We can choose what we remember. So, do we choose to remember what God has done?

> Finally, brothers and sisters, whatever is true, whatever is noble, whatever is right, whatever is pure, whatever is lovely, whatever is admirable – if anything is excellent or praiseworthy – think about such things. Whatever you have learned or received or heard from me, or seen in me – put it into practice. And the God of peace will be with you. (Philippians 4.8–9)

These verses from Philippians are often interpreted through the filter of the present and the future: *be careful what you watch, what you listen to, what you read*. But surely it also refers to what we meditate on in terms of our past? By our actions we choose what we remember, we choose which memories we consolidate, and we choose which memories we allow to fade over time.

Our brains, instead of being dominated by the 'now' worries of each day, can instead be populated and directed by hundreds of stories of what God has done. We can put some really good books in our library; we can fill it with the miraculous and the incredible. We can ensure that our mental real estate is inhabited with amazing accounts of the God who can do anything, a resource to draw from in times of need. The narrative of divine hindsight which each account develops can transform our minds from the stress of the earthly impossible to the freedom of the unlimited possibilities of heaven. And what I find really exciting is that the Bible shows us how we can do this. This is important because the way we respond in times of trial is predicated on the degree to which we have trained our mind and built up our libraries of memory. Scripture shows us a number of techniques to strengthen the chains: immediate consolidation, repetition, authentic consolidation, physical triggers and written accounts.

Immediate consolidation

There is an interesting pattern in the word of God, a sort of refined repetition, which happens time and time again in the Old Testament. Frequently, when God acts, the key protagonist in the story then repeats what God has done immediately afterwards. For example, in the account of the exodus of the Israelites from Egypt, their escape through the waters of the Red Sea is described in Exodus Chapter 14; then in Chapter 15, we find 'The Song of Moses and Miriam', which describes it again.

This happens on multiple occasions in the Scriptures, and if we believe the Bible to be God-breathed (2 Tim. 3.16), then we have to ask why. In the example above, Moses is consolidating the memory of what God has done; he is declaring the truth to those who were there, so the factual miracle is locked down. In the song, he and Miriam are not only praising God but also declaring the truth and reinforcing its memory. I wonder what the Israelites had made of the previous night. They would have been grasped by fear as they passed through the sea, perhaps disorientated by the fierce winds that swirled around them. In the midst of this were the cries of panic from the tribes as they fled to the other side and the roar of the chariots chasing behind them. Then the sounds of the sea crashing down and the screams of the army. And all of this took place in the dark of night. It would be easy across the thousands rescued for there to have been multiple confused experiences and interpretations of what took place, and so it's vital that Moses is able to bring clarity. The detailed and precise song consolidates the memory.

This immediate consolidation and revisiting of it also wards off the introduction of false memories. Though Freud's research shows how emotion can repress memory, contradicting this, Loftus[III] details numerous disturbing accounts of false memories being maliciously planted. In fact, Loftus and her colleague Pickerell[IV] were able over a year to successfully plant in a number of students the memory that they had met Warner Bros' Bugs Bunny on a trip to Disneyland. Though their experiment was not in any way filled with mal-intent, it highlights the importance of securing a memory and ensuring it is impregnable when it comes to memorizing God's work.

It's interesting in so many modern-day miracles where this consolidation of accuracy does not take place how many multiple accounts emerge of what occurred. We see this in the miracle of The Angel of Mons in the First World War, where there is a wide variety in what soldiers on both sides reported. The story goes that as the Prussian army was in advance singing victory songs, they suddenly started firing at a hill where there was no army. The retreating British army could not understand what was happening. Then the Prussian army started to flee in terror. But the accounts of what happened vary. Some say it was angels in chariots that charged the army, some say angelic bowmen were on the hill and German soldiers were found with arrows in them. Another account is of a luminous cloud that hovered there. The general consensus, or could it just be the prominent secular view, is that it is all a complete myth based on a fictional story. The lack of an immediate pulling together of the story has caused even its validity to be questioned, and this is what our heroes in the Bible time and time again avoid by repeating the story of what has just happened.

Repetition

The biblical pattern of repetition for reinforcement shows the importance of capturing and recording the miracle as soon as possible to protect the integrity of the account of God's intervention. The divine strategy is to consolidate the story and to maintain its authenticity against exaggeration and against doubt. I have only ever seen a handful of physical miracles occur before my eyes, and on this occasion immediate consolidation and frequent repetition was essential.

As answered prayers go, this one is slightly embarrassing. Following my time as the chaplain of Leicester City, I got involved with a non-league club and enjoyed being an active member of their part-time staff – which on one occasion meant attending a football game on a Saturday before preaching to five congregations on a Sunday, thus requiring me to be away all weekend. On that Saturday morning, I packed in five minutes – clothes, Bible and toothbrush were thrown into a bag, and I sped off to the game. It was a disappointing match, followed by a post mortem in the club bar, after which I jumped into the car to begin my three-hour drive to the hotel. On arriving at around 11 p.m., I set my alarm for 6 a.m. and let my head hit the pillow. In the morning, I washed, prayed and ran through my notes for the morning ministry. Realizing my clothes would be scrunched up because I'd thrown them in the bag, I decided I should probably give them a quick iron. However, when I pulled my light beige chinos out of my bag, I gasped in horror. I'd packed the wrong ones! This was the pair on which I'd recently spilled a can of Red Bull, resulting in a large dark stain in a rather unfortunate area. Certainly not a place I would want people's attention drawn to while preaching. My initial reaction was to go to reception to see if they had washing facilities on site, but I found the reception was shut and no one on site. I took a few deep breaths and went back to my room; the stain was perfectly inappropriately placed and the size of your average coaster. I wet the top half of the stain with a bit of soap and water, but as I scrubbed, it just got bigger and bigger. At this point, I have now escalated to sheer panic, imagining all five congregations not listening to a word I say but just staring at me for 40 minutes and thinking to themselves, 'I think he's wet himself.'

I didn't know what to do and so I stood there, laying my hand on the stain, and called out to God, 'Jesus, I am so, so sorry. Please forgive my lack of preparation, but please, through your grace and mercy, Lord can you help me?' When I removed my hand, the stain had gone! For the rest of the day, I kept looking at my trousers; did that really happen? Maybe cleaning it with soap and water had done the job? But no, I remembered the details. I only cleaned the top half of the stain, and that whole area of the trousers was wet. After I prayed, they were dry and clean in an instant. Once again, God had been incredibly gracious towards me, and I would never forget it. The following day I sat and recorded the miracle in detail, just to make sure.

My trouser stain story of answered prayer is one of the few times in my life I have seen a physical miracle. Doubt came in almost immediately. I could not believe what my eyes had just seen, so I had to retrace my steps, capture the details and recall them. Talking with others, I found that it's pretty common for unbelief to rapidly attempt to gain a foothold when miracles happen. It is the birds swooping down to steal the seed of faith (Matt. 13.4); it's Peter focusing on the troublesome wind after he takes his first steps on the water (Matt. 14.30). Without the consolidating steps I took, doubt would have inevitably robbed me of the truth and revelation of God which lay within the miracle. There is a responsibility on us to steward the miracle story, to ensure that the memory is properly acquired and that its authenticity and integrity are not weakened over time.

Authentic consolidation

It seems that time has an inevitable impact on the truth. The euphoric emotion that we feel at that moment of miracle is often tempered by the passing of years. The truth we discover of the one who answers can fade, and the knowledge of him who is able can be eroded over time. The dulling of those heightened senses opens the door for the unwanted guest of doubt. The further we travel from that instant of divine intervention, the dimmer our recollection is. I wonder whether the great modern heroes of faith who have fallen from grace would have done so if they could remember with clarity what God had done through them?

One of the dangers for our memories is that any fading over time also leads to distortion. The stories can get damaged, not only through doubt, but sometimes by 'over egging' what happened. The tendency to exaggerate is great, perhaps well illustrated by Yorkshire cricket umpire Dickie Bird. He is probably one of the game's most famous characters and was at his peak in the 70s and 80s. Since then, modern technology has been introduced with the aim of improving umpires' decisions, with the two umpires on the field now supported by a whole team of umpires watching from the stands and surrounded by screens. A natural iconoclast, Bird one day told a cricket commentator how ridiculous it was having all these umpires, as in his day he'd had to umpire a whole test match all on his own. He proceeded to detail how his fellow umpire, in protest at the cricketers' aggression towards him, had walked off the pitch, jumped in his car and driven home in the middle of the match. Bird recalls that he had no option but to continue the rest of the match on his own without a suitable replacement. The commentator who heard Bird's account asked his statistician to verify the story. It was true that Bird's fellow umpire had left in the middle of the competition, never to return. But Bird's claim of umpiring the game on his own for days until a replacement could be found was slightly stretching the truth. The statistician confirmed that Bird had been on his own – for a matter of five whole minutes! Over time, five minutes had evolved into the entire match in Bird's mind. I don't believe he was lying, just that over the decades, exaggeration had taken hold. If doubt can nullify the power of a testimony of what God has done in the heart of the one who experienced it, then exaggeration can similarly nullify any impact of the story on the listener. In the past, I would internally refine some stories of answered prayer, telling myself that this was necessary to make it more palatable to the hearer, that certain details that didn't quite fit could be dropped or moulded. This is wholly inappropriate. In doing so, I was effectively saying, 'Great miracle, Jesus, terrific story, wow! What an ending! Now, if you don't mind, my tiny little brain has thought up some small alterations to make it even better. Then it will really have an impact on people – what do you think, Jesus?'

God does not need our help when it comes to this. To adapt and adjust our answered prayers in any way detracts from what he was revealing through them. As Salvador Dali put it, 'the difference between false memories and true ones is the same as for jewels: it is always the false ones that look the most real, the most brilliant.' So an essential element to the retelling of any divine intervention in our lives is capturing the story as soon and as authentically as possible. Write it, record it, and repeat it, while it is strong in your memory, while the freshness of the experience remains. The all-powerful Lord Jesus Christ needs no exaggeration or embellishment; who can add to the one who is all in all?

Physical triggers

One of the practical ways we can secure memories is through the use of visual prompts. The Bible is full of references to physical triggers which are created to consolidate the memory of God's story in an individual's life. A friend of mine had been praying for finance so that he and his wife could buy their first home. He led a Bible study one day, and one of those present handed him a cheque to pay for his deposit. He wanted to make sure he never forgot what God had done in his life so he placed a large stone by the side of his new driveway. Now, every day when he arrives home, he is reminded of God's miracle provision for him, and he praises God.

In the Scriptures, we see many examples of stones being laid to remember a miracle or encounter with God. In Genesis 28, we see Jacob setting up a pillar to remember God speaking in his dream. At that place, he asked for the protection of God, and he committed to submit to God's lordship and give a tenth of all he had. In a different context, Samuel uses a stone to remember the victory against the Philistines at Mizpah (1 Sam. 7.12) and not only does he set it up, but he also names it *Ebenezer* – 'God of help'. It's important to note that these stones are not idols to be worshipped; they are visual prompts pointing to an unseen God and physical reminders that if he has done it once, he can do it again. These stones were laid down in Gilgal and still seen multiple generations later by Ehud in Judges 3. In other examples, Hagar named a well as a reminder of God's intention and promises (Gen. 16.14). A less obvious physical trigger in the word of God is the staff. In Old Testament times, it was a tradition for a shepherd to make a mark on his staff every time God provided for or protected him[v] – as he walked with his staff, he was walking with the testimonies of God, a constant reminder that God was with him. So when Jacob was 'leaning on his staff' (Gen. 47.31; Heb. 11.21), he was in effect trusting in all that he had seen God do. And the famous Psalm 23 takes on new meaning in this context: 'I will fear no evil, for you are with me; your rod and your staff, they comfort me.' In other words, in the storm right now, I'm going to look at my staff and not let fear take hold, because I can actually see that you are with me.

These physical triggers are invaluable because they can stand outside our current environment. No matter our emotional state, no matter the seriousness of the challenge that may currently engulf us, these visual prompts remind us of a consolidated story that does not change. They can provide stability and security to help us recall who God is, whatever the situation. They make hope visible in those times we cannot see.

We should not limit consolation purely to the sense of sight; smell, touch and sound all can assist us in remembering. Some more clever theologians than I[2] have spotted that when Jesus seeks to re-deem Peter from his rejection of him, it is no coincidence that he does so by a fire on the seashore (John 21). Standing, seeing the flick-ering flames, the crackle of the fire and the smell of burning, Peter's memory of rejecting Jesus in front of the fire in the High Priest's courtyard is triggered (John 18).

Written accounts

The Old Testament writers, the gospels and the apostles' letters all tell us of what God has done so that we may never forget. James D. G. Dunn[VI] describes the gospels as remembrances of Jesus's supernatural authority (words) and power (works). And we are en-couraged also by the psalmist to continue in re-presenting God's works: 'Let this be recorded for a generation to come, so that a peo-ple yet to be created may praise the LORD' (Ps. 102.18, ESV). William Booth, founder of the Salvation Army, wrote in his diary account after account of God intervening to support his calling. Likewise, George Muller was prolific in his recording of God's miracles in his efforts to care for the poor. Let us in the modern day not lose use of this invalu-able methodology to capturing God stories. My wife writes answers to prayer, unexpected provisions and blessings in a small blue book. Over the decades, there have been multiple times when we have called on God for provision and multiple times when he has answered, and the little blue book captures them all. And it's powerful. When we are in the storm of finances, of unexpected bills, or an unexpected loss of income, we read the book. And as I recall the provisions, the blessings, the surprises, a phrase always comes to mind: 'he has never let us down, and there is no reason to believe he will today.' This is the power of consolidation; even when I can't think straight, it enables me to remember the goodness and faithfulness of God in our lives.

---

2   Not a high bar.

We can control the real estate of our mind and what memories are fed into it, and the Bible shows us techniques of consolidation, whether it be immediate repetition and capture, physical triggers or written accounts that ensure that we not only remember the right things but remember them right. These God-inspired books in the libraries of our minds can then be used to full effect guiding us through the worst storms of life when we fear we are going to lose the plot.

Answered prayer: August 1996

Mark and his wife had only been married for a few years and, with a growing family, they were looking to move to a larger house. He was working as an associate pastor of a small church, so was on a very low income. They had spotted a house in the next village that seemed perfect, except for the price. They seemed unlikely to get a look-in, but it also seemed to be the right house, so as we all do when trying to make a decision, Mark oscillated frequently between yes and no. One day, he decided to go to the village where the potential property was located to prayer-walk around the streets. What he really needed was clarity and confirmation from the Lord to give him the peace and security needed to take a leap of faith and go for the house.

As he walked the streets around the house, he wasn't demanding anything from God, just talking to him, telling him how he was feeling. It was then that his attention was drawn across the road to a close-boarded fence running along someone's back garden. It was one of those places where people would pin up posters advertising events and services in the village. But what caught his eye was a lone business card tucked behind the corner of one of the posters. He crossed the street to take a closer look, and to his amazement the card simply had a verse of scripture printed on it from Matthew 8.13: 'You have believed, so it will be done for you.' Why it was there and who had placed it there, he was never able to find out, but Mark believed the Lord had drawn him to it and took it as confirmation!

Mark and his family kept the card as a permanent and special reminder of God's goodness. And yes, he bought the house.

Practical steps

1 Here are some ways you can create physical triggers:

- Create a memory jar. Write down and put in it answered prayers as they happen.
- Take a momento from a story of answered prayer – your own or someone else's – and put it in a place you will see regularly to remind you of who God is.
- Keep a journal and make sure you read back regularly what you have written.
- Take a walking stick and carve symbols on it to represent God moments in your life.

2 Read Joshua 4. Consider some stories from your life that you believe are valuable to capture. Get 12 stones and assign to each one of them a God memory; maybe paint or write one word on them to help you recall each story.

9
Calming the midnight madness

Anxiety flourishes
where fact forces truth
to retreat.

Have you ever noticed that when God is pinpointing an area for improvement in our lives, he does so by highlighting the same issue in multiple settings? The people and places may change, but the subject matter remains the same. Often the pressures that stretch us at work are the same ones that surface at home. A relationship issue where there is a fault in our character can surface with our partner, friends and work colleagues, all perfectly synchronized. When that happens, it's like a letter arriving from God in big red ink, guiding us to deal with it head on. I love the way the Holy Spirit graciously deals with us one thing at a time. He does not overload us with all our shortcomings at once, the letters do not come thick and fast; rather, he masterfully isolates an area for correction before moving to the next. Step by step, we are transformed, fearfully and wonderfully working out our salvation.

I have often received such a 'letter' from God around the subject of faith over fear, particularly in relation to money. Significant money troubles at work have always been coupled with financial struggles at home, and there have been moments when shortfalls in finance have completely dominated my thought life, where every decision I make has been dictated by fear and anxiety, where the fear of tomorrow has overtaken the realities of today. And yet God's provision in our lives has been amazing, and the generosity of God's people when responding to the Holy Spirit's prompting to help us put food on the table each month has been humbling, staggering and miraculous. My accountant friend often freaks out when we discuss the current financial pressures we are under, 'How do you even sleep at night?' Over the years, I have received those 'letters' from God, responded, learnt and developed an approach which enables me even in the most extreme environments to find peace. I sleep well because I remember.

My wife and I started living this way over 18 years ago. Sarah had given birth to our first child, and her maternity leave was coming to an end; she was a junior doctor training to be a GP so was bringing in a good income. I was not. I was starting a software business and planting a church; it was a struggle to generate even a tiny bit of money each month. However, we prayed and felt strongly that God did not want her to return to work but to focus on the family. Sarah was thrilled; I was stressed. The gap we had in our monthly income was significant – I needed my business to take off, but it was hard work and progress was difficult. The next big deal was always just on the horizon, but disappointments arrived one after another. Then, over the weeks, months and years, finance came in. Unexpected cheques, surprise rebates, anonymous money through the door. I remember once getting a wedding invite containing a cheque for us for £1,000! Sarah started to record all these miracles of provision in the previously mentioned small blue book; every blessing was counted and recorded. It seemed insignificant at the time, but her small act of thankfulness was to transform the way I understood my Father in heaven – the great provider, our Jehovah Jireh – and unlock a weapon to fight my greatest fears. One of those euphoric and horrifically scary moments happened for me in the summer of 2019.

Faith for finance

The personal pressure to make ends meet is reaching boiling point; the money from selling my business has long since left the building. Every month during 2019 I've not known how I'm going to pay the bills, not only for my family but also for the charity I run. It's month eight and a miracle that we have made it this far, but I am mentally and emotionally exhausted, continually battling to cope with the pressure of trying to raise money for the project and to pay staff. Sarah and I make the decision that we have to sell our dream house, but I have no idea how we are going to survive financially until the sale goes through. My mind becomes a battleground: on the one side, I have a whirlwind of numbers working out the shortfall; on the other side, I'm strengthened by the power of testimony. I refer to Sarah's little book of answered prayers of provision, and it's a strength to me. I read over and over the dates and amounts of the financial blessings that Jesus has delivered to us, stirring my heart, refreshing my spirit, recalibrating my mind.

In the moments before a prayer is answered, the battle is often at its peak. I've spent the last few weeks trying to find a way to pay the bills; I've tried everything: numerous calls with my bank manager, releasing equity from the house, delaying bills, and bringing income forward and of course lots of worry-dominated prayer. Nothing works. We are once again on the cliff edge.

That morning, I check my bank app, once again battling the numbers: *Well, that's it – I'm stuffed. Just two days until we default on our mortgage, and there is no way out. Jesus, it's over to you now, I can do no more.* And with tears in my eyes, I begin to worship him in the kitchen, remembering all the blessings that are counted in the book. Sometimes I can worship like I'm just singing the words, but on this occasion, I am owning them, meaning them. Each phrase is heavy with purpose. Singing that I will trust in God alone. Soon, faith rises in me. I remember the miracles, the provisions, and that Jesus has never let me down. I recall his intention toward me to be my provider. I feel it's decision time: hold on to the worries, keep up with the mental arithmetic of income vs expenses, wobbling on the edge – or surrender. Strengthened by memories, I jump.

After the surrender, I feel peace. Unbeknown to me, somebody has woken up that morning, turned to his wife and said, 'I think we need to give some money to some people.' Sarah and I are two of the people they feel led to give to that morning, and the money is transferred that day. They had no idea what we were facing, but God did. He always does. In that moment of provision, I felt God grabbing me, reminding me: 'I've got you. I've got your back; it's all going to be ok.' My emotions may have fooled me that God was far away, but he is close all the time.

I'm learning to not only recognize such a moment but to take it as an eternal truth and incorporate it into my being, consolidating it before I can forget or explain away the memory. It is this continuing process of focusing on the essential truth of the story that has equipped me to have faith for more and sleep-filled nights; it heads off panic and banishes what I call the 'midnight madness'.

When fear runs riot

Have you ever had the 'midnight madness'? It's one of those moments that you wake up and in an instant, *that* worry enters your mind. It's the worry that has been nagging away at you, the one that's maybe been pushed to the back of your mind or that you've been distracted from. But now you have woken up, and there it sits, right in front of you, and it has your full attention. And the worry enlarges as you meditate on it. It expands and expands, takes more ground and makes even the most outrageous and severe consequences seem perfectly reasonable. And before you know it, it's 3 a.m., and it feels like the world is about to end. It's the time where the thought of a simple meeting with your boss boards the worry train, and before you know it, it has taken you from an innocuous meeting to an acrimonious sacking, and from there to unemployment, then being unemployable and ultimately homeless. The worry is out of control; it's speeding along and nothing is going to stop it. And in the dawn hours, it seems logical, realistic and terrifying. In the morning, exhausted and wracked with fear, you make your way to work, resigned to face the inevitable doom. As you open the door to your boss's office, she smiles and proceeds to tell you how happy she is with your performance, and you wonder how that worry had seemed so real.

We've all been there, fretting over something that never happens, and the Bible is so straightforward on the issue: 'But seek first his kingdom and his righteousness, and all these things will be given to you as well. Therefore, do not worry about tomorrow, for tomorrow will worry about itself. Each day has enough trouble of its own' (Matt. 6.33). These scriptures are all very well, but when someone delivers them to me in glib fashion, I wish I could smack the person with a fish from Foggy's chip shop![1] So how do we win the battle of worry? How do we jump off the anxiety train in practice?

Transitioning from faith to fear

When we operate in faith, it is based on what we can't see; when we operate in fear, it is based on what we can, or rather what we *think* we can, often constructed from a perspective of facts. It is as unseen as faith, but it feels more real because the facts are more tangible. Faith is unseen, and our trust in it is often reinforced with more of the unseen. I find a focus on facts often just fuels fear. In God's improbable and impossible economy, facts are just a matter of opinion, a point of view, and I can consume them to feed my fear or seek an alternative reality. *We can give you medication that will slow down the disease, but at some point, it's going to spread to your neck. You are overdrawn, and you cannot pay your mortgage tomorrow. Only thirty thousand people were expected to be saved from the beaches of Dunkirk.* All facts, nothing wrong with people saying them, but I believe they are just a matter of opinion, a point of view, an observation on the current state of play. Not one of them accounts for the God who can, and in each of the above, I have seen him act and overcome. In Psalm 77, the writer is undoubtedly succumbing to a bout of the midnight madness, but eventually his eyes see the right answer.

---

1 Foggy's Chip Shop in Worcester. Aptly named after its original owner who cycled around the streets of Worcester, delivering fish while beeping his horn to let the wonderful natives of Worcester know of his arrival. Evidently, it sounded like a foghorn, and so he was nicknamed Foggy. I never saw him on his bike, nor, to be honest, have I ever hit someone with a fish from his establishment.

> I cried out to God for help;
> I cried out to God to hear me.
> When I was in distress, I sought the LORD;
> At night I stretched out untiring hands,
> And I would not be comforted.

I think it's a state we can all relate to, the times when our emotions are so high that our thoughts, fears and doubts are pressing in. In Psalm 56.3–4, we are encouraged when fearful to look to God: 'When I am afraid, I put my trust in you.' James 1.6–7 warns us that our prayers are endangered when we allow ourselves to be blown about by the storms of life. So if facts fuel fear, then recollecting God's deeds fuels faith. How can we see what others can't? Remembering what God has done provides us with the faith fuel we need to achieve anything. Faith for the unseen can be stirred when we look in the right place.

The present day can be filled with lies and tomorrow even more so, but divine truth covers all time and by taking our minds back to the God of the past, we can gain more trust that God holds our future. The psalmist is able to shake off his morose mood by remembering who God is and what he has done. He cannot at that moment directly connect with God, but he transforms his thought process (Rom. 12.2) by recalling who God is, retelling what he has done and singing songs of his deeds. In effect, the psalmist takes himself out of the current environment and moves himself to meditate on his experience, his God experience. God is not viewed in the context of present troubles with perceived doomsday outcomes, nor interpreted through the filter of the psalmist's troubled mind. On the contrary, God is seen through the past, where truth is established over environment, where over time divine realities are set in stone. As Jonah 2.7 recounts: 'When my life was ebbing away, I remembered you.'

The psalmist chooses to view God from past experience, an approach mirrored in Psalm 22. He places his questions, his doubts, his fears alongside the stability of history rather than the present uncertainty. The questions we ask – *Where are you? How could you let this happen? Why can't I hear you? Why are you silent? Why are you not doing things the way I want you to?* – diminish and fade when considered against the backdrop of his miracles in our lives, the lives of others and those recorded in the Scriptures. In effect, all our questions at these times boil down to one: *God, who are you?* Remembering is a powerful tool that ensures we find the right answer.

Recalibration

This movement from present to past in effect brings about a recalibration of the mind. Having access to consolidated memories of God at work allows us to reboot our thinking. The memory of the moment when we experienced divine intervention or the memory in the lives of others allows us to refresh our view of who God is. The eternal truth of our relationship with him is then allowed to pierce through the fog caused by our current challenges and realign our hearts to the knowledge of him. And so by remembering his deeds, we recalibrate our minds to who God is, in the knowledge that he is the God who never changes. And though our current situation may not compute, we humble ourselves (1 Pet. 5.6–7) in the assurance that his ways override our understanding and his past surpasses our present. 'Humble yourselves, therefore, under God's mighty hand, that he may lift you up in due time. Cast all your anxiety on him because he cares for you.' This process is beautifully presented by the psalmist (77.10–12).

> Then I thought, 'To this I will appeal:
>   the years when the Most High stretched
>   out his right hand.
> I will remember the deeds of the LORD;

yes, I will remember your miracles of
    long ago.
I will consider all your works
    and meditate on all your mighty deeds.'

As the psalmist changes his focus and attention from the current ailments to the deeds of the Lord, his view of God is recalibrated. Sensationally, he moves from fear and doubt to awestruck wonder simply through the art of remembering. And then 'Will the LORD reject forever?' (v. 7) is transformed to 'Your ways, God, are holy. What god is as great as our God?' (v. 13). I don't know whether Lauren Daigle's 'Remember' is based on this psalm, but she captures the power of transformation that can take place – moving from a place of pressure where the world's weight is suffocating to a place of unbridled joy and confidence in him.

Weathering the storm –
the continuing story

I wonder what it was like for Paul and Silas following their arrest in Acts 16. In the midnight hour they could have been down, contemplating if now this was the end of their journey, reflecting on whether their own mistakes had got them into this mess. But that is not their reaction. About midnight, Paul and Silas were praying and singing hymns to God, and the other prisoners were listening to them (v. 25). I wonder if in their prayers they recalled what they had already seen God do, what they knew God could do. Is it a jump to suggest that they may have prayed 'God, as you delivered the Israelites, deliver us'? I wonder if their faith rose as they considered the parting of the sea when all they needed was a wall to break down, or maybe they considered the walls of Jericho as they called on God's unlimited strength. We cannot say for certain, but what we do know is the result: 'Suddenly there was such a violent earthquake that the foundations of the prison were shaken' (v. 26). What power lies in remembering? What an incredible tool God has placed in our hands to ward off clouds of doom. Remembering is not a wistful reminiscence, a journey to a safe nostalgic time; rather, it is a weapon which enables us to beat back and win against the very greatest of pressures. We can get through the storms of life by remembering the stories of what Jesus has done. The knowledge of his mighty acts actually equips us to see through any present battle. The testimonies of miracle accounts empower us to overcome the situations we find ourselves in.

I'd love to tell you that I have this absolutely nailed now, that I never hesitate to jump and trust God, and never get on the 'anxiety train'. But that wouldn't be real. What I can tell you is that by disciplining my mind to focus on the past, I find myself increasingly in peace. Even when the stress is at its most extreme, and when those moments of severe stress and anxiety do happen, I am able to recalibrate my thinking most of the time. In all the last six years of trying to build a national landmark about Jesus – with opposition, attacks, hate calls, accusations,[2] and a whole lot of financial shortfall – to date, I have lost sleep no more than three times.

Turning away from the whirlwind

One of the stories of Scripture that helps me rest easy is the account of Peter walking on the water (Matt. 14.22–33). Peter began to sink when his focus moved away from Jesus and towards the ferocity of the storm. It's a simple enough lesson in theory: earthly focus, sink; divine focus, swim. And yet in practice, it can be harder to apply. I remember one particular night where the demands of the charity I lead ran through my head. The anxiety train had arrived: I went from needing to raise over £100k to the charity going bust, losing

---

2 And that just covers the Christian response.

my job, my house, everything, all in the time of a single heartbeat. Against my human urge to worry, I physically rolled over in bed and looked for the 'other' side: I closed my eyes and imagined Jesus standing there on the water. 'God's got this,' I said to myself, and at peace, I fell back to sleep, the midnight madness banished. I choose not to look at the wind for it causes doubt (v. 31) but remember his mighty deeds. He is for me. He is for you.

It has always struck me that the wise man who built his house on the rock and the foolish man who built his house on the sand had much in common – they both faced storms. A life following Jesus is often painted as this skipping-through-the-fields experience, with blue skies and a strong summer sun. *Everything's ok now 'cos you're with Jesus.* And although everything is ok, it is completely outside God's written word to suggest that, somehow, we are not subject to the storms of life. When I decided to follow Jesus in October 1990, did British Telecom write to inform me that now I had 'found the light', they were happy to overlook the red letter demand they had sent and credit my account? Did my Kylie Minogue lookalike girlfriend decide also to give her life to Jesus, marry me and become the perfect wife? Did all my friends and relatives who were sick get instantly healed? No. Of course, none of that happened. The winds still blew, storms still raged. The difference is that I can, like Peter, stand on the water and be part of an incredible, miraculous life and, when the winds blow, turn my head and look to Jesus: he's got this. If I can't see him clearly through the torrent, I recall testimonies of what he has done, until I remember who he is. I don't focus on the storm but on the story maker.

How we remember can have a significant impact on our spiritual walk; the recollection of consolidated memories recalibrates our thinking and puts us back on track when times are rough. But what if you feel like you don't have a modern-day story to recall, reflect on and remember? If you don't have an example of God's power at work in your life today? Well, that's where the rest of us come in. It would be wrong to be fooled into thinking that the art of remembering is a private affair. Scriptures show us that the predominant references to how we remember are in a public context speaking to the assemblies, the households and the families. Indeed, the heart of remembering is wrapped up in the art of storytelling.

Answered prayer: 2006

Rachel's answered prayer may be one of the shortest ever, with the quickest of answers. She had picked up her baby from his cot and went to carry him downstairs. At the top of the stairs, she tripped over one of his brother's toys and went hurtling head first down a full flight of stairs towards a 7-ft floor-to-ceiling glass window at the bottom of the stairs. As her head went past her feet, she knew only Jesus could save them. On instinct, she prayed but never made it past the first syllable of his name: 'Je . . .' Suddenly she found herself sitting at the bottom of the stairs, baby still in her arms, both completely unharmed, the window intact, and not a scratch or a bruise on either of them. Thank God, he hears our heart-prayers as well as the ones we speak out loud.

Practical steps

1 Identify one key area that is a concern/worry at the moment, whether that be health, relationships, finance or something else.
2 Write this at the top of a piece of paper.
3 Find a scripture that relates to this issue, demonstrating that it is within God's will to resolve. Write it down under the heading.
4 Are there any answered prayers in the Bible that relate to this issue? Write these down on the page.
5 Take a moment to think if God has got you through similar situations in the past. If so, write these down in detail.
6 Take some time to find stories from others who have been in similar situations. Talk to friends, read books, go online. Add these to the page.

This page is now your war chest. Whenever you hit doubt or worry about the issue, this page will help you win the battle. Next time the fear hits . . .

7 Write how you're feeling, what is concerning you; write your prayer to God and date it.
8 Reread the scriptures.
9 Reread the answered prayers.
10 Pray for faith.
11 When God answers in his timing, return to this page and capture what happened, thus building your war chest.

10
The art of storytelling

Let this be recorded for
a generation to come,
so that a people yet to
be created may praise
the LORD.
(Ps. 102.18, ESV)

One day my wife asked me if 'Harry's dad' could use our drive for a year to park his car there, adding that he wouldn't mind giving us some money for the space. I said, 'Sure, why not? If he helps us cut down the pear tree, we'll call it quits.' My wife gave me a somewhat quizzical look.[1] We had a 60-ft pear tree close to our house, and every summer it would drop hundreds of pears on the patio, which would then be devoured by swarms of wasps, which rather restricted our time outside. The tree had to go, and this seemed like the perfect opportunity.

The next Saturday, Harry's dad arrived, confidently swinging his chainsaw in hand as he strode into the garden. Sarah's raised eyebrow suddenly made sense. This was not 'Harry's dad', the tree surgeon, but another 'Harry's dad', who was a locksmith. Unfortunately for me, Harry's dad the locksmith was one of those guys who had an un-bounded optimism that he could do anything. At this point I received a little nudge from the Holy Spirit to explain the misunderstanding, give him the parking space and send him on his way. It was a nudge I chose to ignore. Two hours later, and the locksmith has proceeded to lop off every limb of the tree that was keeping it balanced, and the 60-ft monster is now leaning toward the house and Harry's dad is going in for the final cut. I have spent the last two hours nodding like an idiot to his every instruction, while everything within me is telling me to stop. I am holding a rope in the vain hope that my 15 st of muscle and fat[2] can defy the laws of physics and redirect a two-ton tree. I feel the Holy Spirit simply saying *'stop the madness'*, but I'm paralyzed by embar-rassment. I'm praying over and over, 'please help me, Lord' and over and over I hear the Holy Spirit whisper *'stop the madness'*. It seems so simple, but my British aversion to any social awkwardness is now over-riding any sense whatsoever, and I carry on. I grip hold of the rope, brace myself and hope. The locksmith keeps using phrases like 'Don't

---

1   I should know to stop what I'm doing when my wife looks quizzical. You'll see why.

2   Mainly fat.

worry, anything we break we can fix.' That's not helping at all. He tells me that as soon as the tree starts to fall, he will rush over to the rope and grab it with me, and soon after, the tree starts to fall . . . and it's heading for the house. Harry's dad doesn't rush over to grab the rope. He just stands there in shock and swears loudly. Meanwhile, I am unable to defy the laws of physics and engineering and am lifted up off my feet by the tree. In slow motion, I'm flying through the air as I watch a 60-ft pear tree about to demolish my house, and I'm still holding onto the rope. Then, at the last possible moment, the tree twists for no reason a full 90 degrees, just clips the edge of the guttering and misses the house completely. Harry's dad just looks at me and says, 'You were praying, weren't you? I've never seen anything like that in my life.'

It's easy to share the story of that miracle and yet completely miss the point. The house was about to be destroyed, but at the last possible second, the tree twisted. Was it providence? Was it an angel? I'm going for the latter. But as we've already explored, if I'm not careful, I can get lost in the demonstration of God's power and miss his intent. This is a story of God's incredible grace. Grace that overrides utter stupidity, grace that outweighs disobedience, grace that nullifies poor decision-making. Before the beginning of time, God knew this story would happen. He knew the truth I would learn deep down in my soul. He also knows whom I will meet and share this story with so I can tell them about The Giver of grace. My job as a Christian is to reveal the Father, and if I focus in my storytelling on the *why* rather than the *what*, the *who* rather than the *how*, then I can share with the listener eternal insights into the nature of the Father.

The responsibility of storytelling

I've covered in this book the care that needs to be taken in the capturing of such stories as detailed above: pointing to the giver, revealing his nature, focusing on the why, prophesying for it to happen again. But all of this is for naught if the story is evermore untold. The purpose behind the gift of answered prayer is not merely for personal benefit but that in our wise stewarding of it, we take every opportunity to share it and proclaim the nature of God. The context of 'Freely you have received; freely give' in Matthew 10.8 is in respect to freedom from sickness and demon possession, but I contend that the principle can be transposed for all gifts from God. As Christians, we have a generational responsibility to ensure these stories and the thousands like them are preserved.

Generational responsibility

One of the most impressive things about the Jewish nation, for me, is their adherence to the commission from God to 'remember the days of old; consider the generations long past. Ask your father and he will tell you, your elders, and they will explain to you' (Deut. 32.7). Each year at the Passover celebration meal known at the Passover Seder, the story of the exodus is retold, fulfilling God's command in Exodus 13.8, 'On that day tell your son, "I do this because of what the LORD did for me when I came out of Egypt."' Interestingly, the text used for the Seder is called the Haggadah, meaning 'the telling', and because it's written down, the story never changes as it's retold and passed down through the generations. Every element of the Seder is saturated with symbolism, with each element pointing towards remembrance. In this tradition, the youngest son in the room asks the eldest man to share the story, and a ritual proceeds where the younger asks his elder to explain the Passover symbols. Thus each year, year after year, decade after decade, and from generation to generation, the story is passed down. Oh, for the modern Western church to capture this practice of the old telling the young of his mighty deeds.

Throughout the Scriptures, we see the encouragement, commitment and responsibility to ensure that the deeds of the Lord are passed down the generations. In reference to the mighty deeds of the Lord, the psalmist commits, 'We will not hide them from their descendants; we will tell the next generation' (78.4) and a promise to ensure 'with my mouth I will make your faithfulness known through all generations' (89.1). Just two examples from a long list in Scripture of the emphasis on our responsibility to communicate through the generations. As we build a long-lasting intimacy with Christ, we should be able to build on the foundation of understanding, revelation and experience from those who have gone before us, and as Judith Ude[3] says, 'Pass it on.' We're incredibly privileged to have a Bible where we can read of the things that God has done, and blessed to have the freedom to study the intricacies of his word. We can read about his deeds and understand who he is. But more than that, we can learn from the lives of the heroes of our faith and read about their sacrifices and adventures with the Lord. I believe every story captured and recorded and shared with our descendants lays a foundation for more of God to be experienced and more of his power in action to be seen for the days to come. We have a generational responsibility to share that he is still, and always will be, the God who can and the God who does. 'Future generations will be told about the LORD. They will proclaim his righteousness, declaring to a people yet unborn: He has done it!' (Ps. 22.30–31).

And every story shared, every testimony told, declares not only his ability but his love for the current generation: 'But the plans of the LORD stand firm forever, the purposes of his heart through all generations' (Ps. 33.11). Remembering in Scripture and tradition is not passive; it's not purely a cognitive reflection. The word of God is clear when it refers to remembering his deeds, using words like 'tell', 'proclaim', 'declare', 'announce'. Remembering is active; it is communicative. And it is to the next generation that we need to communicate.

---

3 Just absolutely love this song as it captures the heart of this whole book. Judith Ude – 'Hope in Stone/Pass it on'.

Telling the next generation

So how do we do it? How do we preserve the story? We've already looked at the various ways the Bible suggests we consolidate our stories, but for now, let's look a little closer at the life of Joshua. In Joshua 4, God instructs the Israelites to memorialize the fact that he has parted the river for them to cross. Joshua asks each tribe to take a stone from the riverbed, 12 in total, for the purpose of building a monument to help them remember what God has done.

> So Joshua called together the twelve men he had appointed from the Israelites, one from each tribe, and said to them, 'Go over before the ark of the LORD your God into the middle of the Jordan. Each of you is to take up a stone on his shoulder, according to the number of the tribes of the Israelites, to serve as a sign among you. In the future, when your children ask you, "What do these stones mean?" tell them that the flow of the Jordan was cut off before the ark of the covenant of the LORD. When it crossed the Jordan, the waters of the Jordan were cut off. These stones are to be a memorial to the people of Israel forever.' (Josh. 4.4–7)

It's interesting that at this moment, Joshua's focus was on consolidating the story for the following generations, perhaps with the hindsight of how easily those delivered from Egypt had forgotten previously the God who delivered them. They carry the stones to Gilgal and set them up there. In v. 21, Joshua instructs them that when their descendants ask why the stones are there, they are to tell them not only the story of what God did, but also what that story tells us about God:

> He did this so that all the peoples of the earth might know that the hand of the LORD is powerful and so that you might always fear the LORD your God. (v. 24)

I imagine that these stones became a focal point for the city of Gilgal, that its elders would sit and tell the stories of what God did in that incredible journey to the Promised Land, and tell the children listening that he is the God who never changes.

Over a hundred years later, the stones are having an impact. The Israelites are subject to King Eglon of Moab, but they cry out to God, who sends Ehud to deliver them. Ehud met with King Eglon, whom he intends to murder, but doesn't go through with it. As he returns from this meeting, Ehud comes across 'stone images' at Gilgal (Judg. 3.19). It's interesting that the word of God highlights this. Ehud then dismisses his advisors and returns to assassinate the king. It is widely thought that these stones were graven images, idols. It's my opinion that as he looked on the stones, he remembered Joshua's stones at Gilgal, remembered the story of God's deliverance, and remembered the meaning of the story: God's power. I sense that Ehud was reminded to fear only God and returned to kill the king and deliver the people. The point in the context of answered prayer is that the story of the stones is known; it's still alive in God's people.

Joshua 4 is perhaps the scripture that best explains why I'm involved in a project to build a monument representing a million answered prayers – so that the generations would be inspired to remember the goodness of God, the power of God and the protection of God.[4] Putting stories of what Jesus has done into this monument is a great way to record and preserve them for our descendants, but although this is a unique opportunity, there are other practical ways in which we can preserve the Jesus history we enjoy. The way we can change the country is not by merely creating physical reference points to God's deeds, but by changing the Christian culture and becoming a nation of storytellers.

---

4   It's worth mentioning that we are not looking for this modern-day monument to inspire regicide! I love our monarchy and the times they have prayed for our nation.

Remembering in the covenant meal

In Scripture, there is a clear instruction from Jesus, which is to remember him as we partake of it.

> 'This is my body, which is for you; do this in remembrance of me.'
> In the same way, after supper he took the cup, saying, 'This cup is the new covenant in my blood; do this, whenever you drink it, in remembrance of me.' (1 Cor. 11.24–25)

Too often, Holy Communion is seen as a sombre affair. It is true that when we partake of it, we should reflect on that incredible sacrifice on the cross, and we should also reflect on the Christ who rose again. It is the most significant moment in history; it should be remembered. But how else should we remember him and how should this be outworked in the covenant meal? From my experience of travelling around churches, the Lord's Table is largely defined by the remembrance of an historical Jesus, not the one we know today. It is rare that the Jesus of the present or even previous generation is remembered; his deeds and nature are not recalled, in preference for an exclusive focus on that glorious day when our eternities were transformed. If we are to remember him in fullness, then we should consider widening our scope at such times. Nowadays, I not only reflect and give thanks for the miracle that changed the world for ever, I also take the opportunity to remember the times that I and others have called on his name and he has answered. I understand that in many Christian traditions, Holy Communion is a formal practice undertaken during a service, but I long to see a time when, whether in meetings or around dinner tables, families and friends take the bread and wine while they share their stories of answered prayer. Could we proclaim his death and resurrection until he comes by encouraging each other with stories of who he is, what he is like?

> Whenever you eat this bread and drink this cup, you are retelling the story, proclaiming our LORD's death until he comes. (1 Cor. 11.26, TPT)

What would family life be like if, as well as a traditional prayer of thanks for food, testimonies were told around the table of first-hand accounts of the power of God? What if our coffee shops, schools, shops and workplaces were filled with people gossiping about the things their eyes had seen of the God who answers? In whatever way we choose to remember, ultimately moving our forgetful culture from historical religious observance to awesome remembrance will be achieved by individuals deciding to incorporate this wholesome tradition into their lives. Have the generations below you heard your stories? I've heard my friend use the phrase, 'What are your 12 stones?' effectively asking: tell me 12 stories of God's deeds. They may not all be yours – some may be captured from history – but they should be easy to hand if we are to create a Christ-sharing storytelling culture. To become a nation of storytellers, to share our stories with each other, with our children and their children, will require a resolute spirit. And to do so, we have to overcome a very real challenge that is imposing itself on the body of Christ. Western society is increasingly creating a culture where such stories are unwelcome, where truth is being eradicated and Jesus stories silenced. Let us not succumb to this pressure nor allow ourselves to be squeezed into a mould where the church is on mute.

Answered prayer: around 550 AD

During St Columba's time in the Picts province, one man heard him preach, and his whole household believed and turned to Christ. A few days later, one of his sons became gravely ill. At the time, some heathen witches, on seeing the boy beginning to die, mocked the followers of Christ, pointing to their own gods and belittling Jesus. On hearing this,

St Columba was moved and set off to the young boy's house. When he arrived, the boy had passed away. He asked the father where the body lay and was led to it. Entering alone, he went to the body, knelt, wept and prayed. After some time, he was then heard crying out, 'In the name of the Lord Jesus Christ, wake up again and stand upon thy feet.' The boy's eyes opened and St Columba raised him to his feet and took him back to where his parents mourned, and the celebrations began.

Practical steps

1 Why not try and identify '12 stones' in your life or in the life of others? Recollect and collect 12 stories of the things God has done in your life or in history or in a friend's life. Learn them well; ensure they are accurate. Pray for opportunity to tell one of them.

2 When you next meet with a friend, ask him or her to share a story of how God has moved in his or her life and encourage the friend to pass on this story to at least one more this week.

3 When you meet in a small group, why not have a time together to share stories of God at work in your life this week and the opportunities you've had to share them?

4 Ask your children and youth workers if one day they could invite older generations to come in and tell stories of his marvellous deeds.

5 Why not have an annual feast with your family as an excuse to tell stories of what God has done in the family over the years?

11
Church on mute

Tolerance of others
should not translate
to the silence of self.

I love Emeli Sande's 'Read All About It Part III'. I don't know if she's a Christian, but when she sings about having words that can change a nation, and that our fear-driven silence prevents people hearing our song, it causes me to think about spiritual remembrance and why I should never be silent about what God has done, not only in the Church but outside of it. Ultimately, our great commission is to 'make disciples', and storytelling is central to that; it's one thing to tell someone what Christians believe, another thing to share why we, personally, choose to put our trust in Jesus. Our real-life stories carry power – indeed, it's not by accident that the use of parables was Jesus's modus operandi when communicating to the masses.

Telling Jesus stories

I'm not suggesting that testimonies have any superiority over the inspired word of God. The Bible is the framework within which we live; it is a picture frame we cannot add to, and we are forbidden from extending the size of the canvas. But within this frame, sharing first-hand experiences of the Jesus who answers can give greater insight to the listener and a validity which could empower them to discover the Lord of our life.

When I was chaplain of Leicester City Football Club, I had the great privilege of meeting and spending time with Sven Goran Eriksson, the former England manager who at that time was managing the Leicester team. If you Google him, you'll find a wide range of opinions and, of course, tabloid gossip. When people find out that I worked with him, we often have interesting conversations – some assume from what they've read in the media that he's very ego-driven, hungry for fame and arrogant. That was not my experience. Behind the scenes, I discovered him to be quite the opposite. Over a period of a few months, we only had a handful of conversations,[1] but one thing really stood out as I saw him interacting with people. He was constantly surrounded by the media, agents or hangers-on who wanted some reflected glory, but on more than one occasion, I would see him cross the room to talk to the person that everyone else ignored. I saw him ignore footballers with European fame to shake the hand of a laundry lady and ask her how she was doing. I once experienced it first-hand when, noticing me from the corner of his eye, he brushed aside the money men and made a beeline to come and chat with me and thank me. Here's the question: when I talk to people about this, why does my account have more credibility than a newspaper report? Why does hearing it 'from the horse's mouth' have more power than reading it or getting a recorded version of events? Perhaps we are programmed to respond more favourably to first-hand accounts from trustworthy sources. This predisposition of human nature towards reliable sources is an open door of opportunity for a story of answered prayer, a remembered story of Jesus at work.

If I share with somebody the facts of the story of the historical Jesus who died, was crucified and then rose from the dead, sometimes I can see people glaze over. They don't hear about the man Jesus; they hear religion and all the trappings that come with it; they hear church and all the misconceptions that come with that too. But if I give them a first-hand account of what Jesus is like, if I tell them stories of my experiences with him, journeying with him and listening to him, it has more credibility. Once I was driving a couple of football players back from a game. 'What's so special about this Jesus bloke then?' asked one. I not only shared the Scriptures, but personal testimonies of what Jesus has done in my life. By the end of the journey, they both asked for more on our next journey, fascinated by what they had heard and never been taught at school.

---

1 One of which included me trying to explain to him the rules of cricket – it didn't go well.

Church on mute

In my project to collect a million stories of answered prayer, I was once accosted by a lady who said, 'I understand that God answers prayer – it has happened to me – but why do you have to brag about it?' I kept my counsel, but I wanted to point to the hundreds of scriptures that tell me to do so. The mantra 'we mustn't talk about answered prayer because it may offend those who have not had their prayers answered' is an approach soaked in the philosophy of political correctness, founded on the fear of offence, and which is completely contradictory to a significant weight of Scripture. As C.S. Lewis states, 'In such a fearful world, we need a fearless church.' And yet countless times, I've had meetings with Christian organizations where the leader has been very positively disposed to the project, only to come back and explain in apologetic tones that there wasn't an appetite among the team. Often only one individual had expressed these PC concerns, yet it had swayed the decision. It leaves me thinking that the Church yet again has been so squeezed into the world's mould that, from genuine motivations of compassion and love, it has in effect silenced itself and we find ourselves with a church on mute.

Opposing opposition

There are many Christians across the world that do things that I am not comfortable with and would not do myself. These may be approaches used by different churches, different theologies that organizations promote or enforce, or groups of Christians that rally around a certain cause. There are things that are done in the name of God with which I simply disagree, but here's the rub: what right do I have to make that judgement? Do I have any standing of significant wisdom over anyone else that should give my viewpoint any more credence than theirs? Furthermore, do I have any right to say what God is in or what God is not in? In short, I believe that the day I gave my life to our Lord Jesus and submitted to him, I surrendered the right to oppose any part of the body of Christ. I believe that, as Christians, we should focus on what God has called us to do and be accountable to go for that.[2] I think this situation is best summed up by Gamaliel in Acts 5.38. He says (TPT version): 'In this situation, you should just leave these men to themselves. For if this plan or undertaking originates with men, it will fade away and come to nothing. But if this movement is of God, you won't be able to stop it. And you might discover that you were fighting God all along!' For each Christian project and philosophy that raises my eyebrows, I simply say, 'If God is in it, it will prosper and if not, it will fade,' and then I crack on with the things that he has asked me to do.

Political correctness

Political correctness seeks to create a world where no one is offended. It looks to create an environment where no one is upset, no one is insulted and no one's feelings are hurt. It seeks to defend the oppressed and ensure that minorities are not overlooked or offended by actions and language. But it's just not possible to achieve, because there are two people involved in any PC conflict, the speaker and the hearer; the one who does the action and the one who is affected by the action. If I proudly post my daughter's A-level results, is it wrong if it offends parents who are upset with their children's grades? The fundamental problem with this approach is that it focuses all its disapproval on the one who offends and leaps instinctively to the defence of the offended.

The Bible deals with both the offender and the offended. In Luke 17, Jesus states that offence is unavoidable (v. 1), an inevitable

---

2   And to avoid the risk of being a hypocrite and criticizing those who criticize, I also recognize that there are some who are called to present well-formed arguments and shape Christian thinking. This, though, I believe is a unique and rare calling.

consequence of the fall perhaps. 'Things that cause people to stumble are bound to come, but woe to anyone through whom they come.' This at first look seems to strengthen the PC brigade's cause, but is in the context of sin, i.e. if we sin and cause others to sin, we are in deep doo-doo.[3] He then warns the disciples not only to be wary of offending anyone but also, critically, not to be offended themselves. 'Even if they sin against you seven times in a day and seven times come back to you saying "I repent," you must forgive them' (v. 4). We are called to forgive seventy times seven times, and our posturing should be one of forgiveness and compassion, not one of holding onto hurt. In Christ, we can decide not to keep open the wounds caused by others' words and actions, to clear the way for the sake of the gospel. If that's the case, then how should we respond when someone acts with good intentions, in line with Scripture to share the gospel? Sometimes the offence we feel can reveal our own displacement before God, rather than that of the offender's. We saw this in Chapter 4 in reviewing the response of the prodigal son's brother to the 'charismata'.

In fact, our response to offence can bring glory to God. If we choose to not be offended and overlook any slight aimed toward us, we bring glory to ourselves and our Father in heaven (Prov. 19.11). When I have faced opposition for doing what I feel God has called me to do, I have a decision to make – feel sorry for myself or pray for the accuser. I am in Christ, and the accuser doesn't necessarily understand who Jesus is and therefore who I am. The emotion of offence is a decision, and the divine strategy is to create a people who are prepared to choose not to accept it in preference for the love of the offender. And so, what should our approach be when we hear a miraculous story that offends us? Are we in the wrong or is the person who told us the story the 'offender'?

There are plenty of scriptures that encourage us not to offend: 'Be careful, however, that the exercise of your rights does not become

---

3 Luke 17.1 Gamble paraphrase version!

a stumbling block to the weak' (1 Cor. 8.9). Further warnings in Luke 17.1, 2 Corinthians 6.3 and Romans 14.13 all point in the same direction: let us not offend. This may add weight to the PC approach: *don't do or say anything that will upset someone, don't share a story of a healing from cancer in case someone has lost someone from the same disease.* But if we read the scriptures in such a way, we are guilty of selective interpretation, because in all these warnings, the danger is that our 'offence' is a stumbling block to the gospel. We should clear the path of any possible hindrances in our communication, ways and traditions so that people can hear the good news without any cultural practices getting in the way. Let's be careful in what we do and say so people can hear the Jesus truth. But if when they hear the Jesus truth, it insults, hurts or upsets, that's all right, they can take it up with him. 'But we preach Christ crucified: a stumbling block to Jews and foolishness to Gentiles' (1 Cor. 1.23).

The only context in which there is a rebuke for offence is when it prevents the sharing of the gospel – the good news story of Jesus. To say we should not tell the stories of what Jesus has done because it will cause offence and stop people hearing the story of Jesus is clearly a nonsensical standpoint from a scriptural basis. In truth, this PC approach which has seeped into the Church of Christ predominates not where it is motivated by love or a fervent passion for the gospel to be unfettered, but often where there is a fear of man. Where there is a fear of the difficult questions that the Jesus stories will raise, the challenge they bring. Jesus was offensive to the religious norm because his very presence, the very knowledge of him, raised a singular question over humanity's reason for existence. Every question that was asked of Jesus essentially had the underlying question 'Who are you?' And if the answer was God, then it would mean ripping up the religion which he opposed. His answers were challenging and even insulting to some, and as the German theologian Dietrich Bonhoeffer observed, such was the level of affront to the religious people in New Testament times that they

154

decided to kill the question. We must not, cannot, allow the offence of the gospel to be silenced in this time because it does not fit
in with the PC culture. Press the unmute button, Church, and let's
be bold and tell stories of what Jesus has done. Let the question be
raised not buried.

Raising the stories

It is, I believe, nigh on impossible to share a story about what God
has done on a wide scale without it upsetting someone. 'Why
didn't God answer that prayer for me?' Someone's understanding
and perceptions of God will inevitably be challenged in the telling. And yet the vast majority of the biblical references that talk
about sharing God's deeds are in the context of a population not an
individual – declaring to the nations, proclaiming to the assembly,
singing to the peoples. The amount of Scripture is significant: well
over one hundred verses encourage us to tell of God's mighty deeds
and miracles to the masses.

There is simply no justification, no reasoning or excuse, for the
Church to do anything other than tell the nation what God has done
and tell it loud. In response to the lady who asked why we have to
brag about it at the public consultation, the answer is simple: because verse after verse instructs us to tell of the wonderful deeds of
God. It is not a private matter. Sure, we see examples of individual
retelling, Daniel informing the king (Dan. 4.2), 'It's my pleasure to
tell you about the miraculous signs and wonders that the most high
God has performed for me,' being just one. But whether it be to individuals or the masses, the theme remains – don't hesitate to tell people what God has done.

Honouring the body

In 2007, one of my best friends died of leukaemia. He was a complete rascal of a bloke, and we thought he would never marry, but he found the love of his life and tied the knot in February 2007. He asked me to say a few words at the wedding, which was a big deal as he was not a believer and hated all the 'Bible stuff'. Towards the end of his honeymoon, he started getting symptoms and was admitted to hospital. I visited him every week and prayed for him, but never with him. In December of the same year he passed away, and I was asked to take the funeral. I don't know why he died, and I don't know why the God who answers didn't say yes. At the wake, one of my friends came up to me and said, 'So much for your God!' It hurt then and it still hurts now.

There is a great joy when you hear the story of something God has done, when you hear of his marvellous deeds. I love those times when friends sit around and excitedly start swapping stories; they are times when your faith gets built so much, and it's good to share with the storyteller's joy, enthusiasm and increased experience of who God is. We revel together in the delight of knowing the God of the impossible. But what happens when I hear a story of healing from leukaemia? It's a bruise that stings immediately, as the memories of my friend's final day come flooding back, sitting by his hospital bed, holding his cold hand. In that moment, I have a choice. I can allow my mind to race: *why is this a story of healing, while mine is one of failure? Why didn't you listen, God? Why didn't you act?* And so on, the traps of comparison, cynicism, anger all lying in wait. Or I can choose to rejoice in hearing a story of healing. 1 Corinthians 12.26 makes the right choice clear: 'If one part suffers, every part suffers with it; if one part is honoured, every part rejoices with it. Now you are the body of Christ, and each one of you is a part of it.' In other words, as others have stood with me in my pain, I will stand with them in the joy of their blessings and aim to share in it as if it were my own. Clearly, there is a sensitivity in sharing these stories; speaking the truth in love is important, and we should deliver such testimonies with care, but that is a different approach altogether to muting the story.

I lost my friend to leukaemia at the age of 40, and I miss him dearly, but I will *decide* how I react to stories of healing on the matter. I will be accountable to God in my response. But which well-meaning person has the right to rob me of hearing stories of joyful accounts of leukaemia being healed? I still sometimes feel I have been robbed of this special friendship; I will not allow anyone to also rob me of enjoying testimonies of healing from the same disease my friend suffered. If one part of the body is rejoicing, I want to stand and rejoice with them. As my mother-in-law says, 'I cannot receive something from God and deny it to another.'[4]

Unmuting

In this postmodern era, we stand in a time which is crying out for truth, and at the same time, through distraction and suppression, doing its damnedest to ensure nobody speaks it. Church, let's wake up, smell the coffee and take every opportunity for the sake of the gospel to declare the deeds of the Lord. My part in God's great tapestry of adventure for us all has been to embark on a journey of collecting a million answered prayers.[5] My intention is to build a Christian national landmark placed in the heart of the nations of the United Kingdom, where each of the million bricks will have captured in them a story of answered prayer. It will last for generations, like the 12 stones at Gilgal, declaring the works of the Almighty. It will not be PC; it will be bold in its statement that Jesus is alive, he listens and he

---

4   I think she got that from somebody else, but she can't remember who!

5   If I haven't inspired you to share your story of answered prayer by now, I probably need to rewrite this book. But if I have, please, please declare your story to the generations and share it at <www.eternalwall.org.uk>.

answers prayer. The journey that I and others have taken to achieve this has been saturated with miracles, gobsmacking moments and a heart-stopping rollercoaster. And my hope and prayer is that the Church becomes brave again, prepared to upset and even insult for the sake of the gospel.

We cannot afford to allow the Church to be squeezed into a mould that seeks to tiptoe around issues, to keep our heads down and not offend anyone. That approach is not represented in Jesus's ministry, and neither should it be replicated in ours. I believe God wants us to be a nation of storytellers, fearlessly and unashamedly sharing accounts of the things that he has done in our time and before. We should declare his deeds to kings and crowds, in assemblies and in conversations, the testimonies of the deeds he has done and is doing around us. Church, it's time to press the unmute button, not only for now but for the generations to come. Let's remember.

Answered prayer: 12 July 2018

Joel and Rachel are on holiday with extended family in Cyprus. Part of the leadership team in their local church, they are passionate about Jesus. Joel has this thing he calls 'The Jesus Experiment', which essentially explores what will happen if he uses the name of Jesus as often as he can. On this particular day, Joel and Rachel are arguing, and Joel feels the most unlike Jesus he has ever felt. As they walk around the capital city, admiring the architecture, Rachel's mum – also on the holiday – is giving Joel a talking to as tensions between Joel and Rachel continue to flare. By the afternoon, it's boiling hot, but before they can head back to the villa, they see a huge mosque and go inside to have a look. 'God, are you here?' Joel prays and feels the Holy Spirit reply, 'My presence is always with you.'

Leaving the mosque, Joel sees a young man sitting on a bench with a cast on his leg. He's in his early 20's, from Syria, and in pidgin English, the two of them start to converse. Joel learns a bit of the

man's story of fleeing the war, getting to Cyprus and the challenges of finding work, exacerbated by breaking his ankle yesterday. Joel
then asks if he can pray for the man's leg in the name of Jesus. The
young man explains that he is a Muslim and doesn't believe in the
power of Isa (Jesus). Joel says that's okay, you don't need to believe;
Jesus will still answer. So the man agrees, saying, 'Well, what have I
got to lose?' Joel places his hand on the cast and says, 'Be healed in
the name of Isa; let this man see that there is no other name than the
name of Isa.' He asks the man to stand and try to put weight on it.
The man can't believe it – the pain has nearly all gone! He starts to
shout to his friends to come over, telling one to get some scissors so
he can cut the cast off. He does so, and Joel prays for him again, for
the pain to go completely.

A crowd from the mosque is starting to gather. The man can't believe it and starts jumping up and down on the leg. Another friend
comes up and asks Joel to pray for his knee. Joel does the same, again
in Isa's name. This man is healed instantly. The crowd increases as
more refugees gather around him. A man with one leg shorter than
the other asks for prayer. Joel sits him down and straightens the man's
legs horizontal to the bench; people now have their phones out, filming. As Joel tells him about the power of Isa, the guy starts freaking
out as his leg is growing and Joel didn't even have a chance to pray!

Then out of the mosque comes a man who starts mocking Joel,
telling him he is wrong, that there is no power in the name of Isa. 'Isa
is just a prophet, my brother. Heal the pain in my side if Isa is so powerful!' he laughs. Joel places his hand on the man's side and prays.
The mocking man's expression changes from laughter to shock; he
stares at Joel and walks away. Joel decides it's time to move on as his
in-laws are waiting on the edge of the crowd for him. He catches up
with Rachel and apologizes to her for his attitude, and they rejoice
together in what God has done.

Two days later, the family are on the Paralimni beach, relaxing
and enjoying the sun. But Joel is bored. He decides to go for a

walk and then to snorkel in the sea, though he is not a great swimmer. Rachel is catching the rays when suddenly she hears a blood-curdling, guttural scream. The busy, bustling holiday-makers stop in their tracks, and the beach falls silent. Rachel's immediate thought is Joel and his swimming ability. *Oh my word, what has happened?* She gets up to see Joel standing waist deep in the sea, unmoving, frozen to the spot.

Moments before, a young girl had been playing in the sea and noticed a man sort of hovering beneath the water. After a few minutes, she returns to the beach and says to her father, 'Daddy, that man has been under the sea for ages. What is he doing?' Instinctively, Loizus, a Greek Cypriot, jumps to his feet, sprints into the water and drags the lifeless body out of the sea. The man is in his early sixties, and as Loizus turns him onto his back, he sees white foam all around the man's mouth; he wipes it clean to reveal blue lips. Another man screams for help.

Joel can't move; he's paralyzed with shock. Loizus's wife, Kendra, jumps into action and starts CPR immediately. A crowd gathers; pin-drop silence disturbed only by the gentle breaking of the waves. After a minute or two, the lifeguard arrives with a defibrillator, but it's chaos – either it doesn't work or it's not charged properly, so he rushes off to get an alternative from a nearby beach. The man's wife is kneeling by his side, sobbing uncontrollably; his daughter stands motionless in shock. Kendra continues with the CPR. Ten minutes pass, which seem like hours, and the defibrillator hasn't arrived. The crowd is starting to slowly drift away, disturbed by the uncomfortable story that is playing out before them. Silence. Kendra has now been doing CPR for ten minutes, so she's tiring. Joel steps up. Soon he starts performing CPR, although he's never done it before. Kendra has moved to the man's feet and, unbeknown to Joel at that time, she is holding them and praying to Jesus. The CPR isn't working, and so Joel, not knowing what else to do, reaches his hand down to the still body, touches its side and screams, bellowing with all that he has, 'IN

JESUS'S NAME I SPEAK LIFE UNTO YOUR BODY! BODY, COME TO LIFE RIGHT NOW.'

The body jolts, and the man begins to breathe. Joel jumps to his feet, 'Yes, Jesus, c'mon!' he screams. The beach cheers. 'You all saw what happened,' Joel proclaims to those still watching, and the whole beach within earshot. 'That was Jesus, that wasn't me! You tried mouth-to-mouth, you tried chest compressions, you tried a defibrillator, but nothing worked. But when I said the name of Jesus, this man came back to life!' More cheers. The wife of the man flung her arms around Joel, thanking him over and over. Then people started coming to Joel, congratulating him and asking him if he could pray for them too, and many are healed.

Later that night, Joel is so pumped that he can't sleep. His mind is racing – did that really happen? Was it the CPR that brought him back? The doubts are running wild. He goes down to the beach the following day and asks the lifeguard what happened. The lifeguard is quizzical; *how could he have forgotten?* 'Er . . . mate,' he begins. 'You prayed for a guy who was dead, shouted at Jesus and he came back to life. What do you mean, what happened?'

Practical steps

1 *Remember* what God has done, *then tell* the world.

Notes

I Have we forgotten to remember?

I Ericsson, Krampe, and Tesch-Roemer, 'The Role of Deliberate Practice in the Acquisition of Expert Performance', *Psychological Review*, Vol. 100 (01 Jul 1993) 363–406.

II Betsy Sparrow, Jenny Liu, and Daniel M. Wegner, 'Google Effects on Memory: Cognitive Consequences of Having Information at Our Fingertips', *Science,* Vol. 333, Issue 6043 (05 Aug 2011) 776–778.

III <https://www.techdirt.com/articles/20110119/05022912725/fifteenth-century-technopanic-about-horrors-printing-press.shtml>

IV D. M. Wegner, T. Giuliano, and P. Hertel, 'Cognitive Interdependence in Close Relationships'. In W. J. Ickes (Ed.), Compatible and Incompatible Relationships (New York: Springer-Verlag, 1985), 253–276.

V Jay Shetty featured in Nihal Arthanaayake Show, BBC Five Live Radio, 3:58pm 15/6/20.

3 The forgotten giver

I 'Fabrice Muamba: Devoted Father and Footballer'. *Sky News*, (18 March 2012).

II L. E. Torrance, *The Plain Truth – Hitler's Seven Fatal Blunders*, (1961) 10.

III David E. Gardener, *The Trumpet Sounds for Britain*, (Jesus is Alive Ministries, 2003).

IV Winston S. Churchill, *The Second World War*, (Bloomsbury).

V <https://www.youtube.com/watch?v=LIQ4qlPbyy8>

4 Disposable trinkets or eternal gifts?

I See Pete Greig, *God on Mute,* (David Cook Publishing).

7 Are you an again believer?

I Bill Johnson, *Power of Testimony.*

8 Choosing to consolidate our God memories

I Chai M. Tyng, Hafeez U. Amin, Mohamad N. M. Saad, and Aamir S. Malik*, 'The Influences of Emotion on Learning and Memory', *Frontiers Psychology.* 8:1454 (2017; published online 24 Aug 2017).

II Tamara Thompson, (Leicester: Chroma Church).

III Elizabeth F. Loftus and Katherine Ketcham, *The Myth of Repressed Memory.* (St. Martin's Press, 1994).

IV E. F. Loftus, 'Make-believe memories', *American Psychologist*, 58:11 (2003), 867–873.

V Thought from Carl Brettle, (Neighbourhood Prayer Network).

VI James D. G. Dunn, 'Jesus Remembered', *Christianity in the Making*, Vol. 1.

Hope is made visible when we **remember**

Eternal Wall is a Christian national landmark.
Opening in 2022 near Coleshill, Birmingham.
Constructed of 1 million bricks
each representing a story of answered prayer.

Share your story at
eternalwall.org.uk/testimony

Share an answered prayer
Help us

MAKE HOPE VISIBLE